This page intentionally left blank

contributors

### JP HOLESWORTH
*Copy Editor and Columnist for Guitar Connoisseur/Blogger*

JP Holesworth has authored Stratoblogster Guitar Blog since 2006. He lives in the Pacific Northwest, subsisting mainly on berries, Nutella and local India Pale Ales. When not writing, cooking or playing guitar he can sometimes be seen hiking the hills south of Kennewick, WA, searching the skies for Stratocaster shaped cloud formations.

**www.stratoblogster.com**

### PASQUALE "PAT" BIANCULLI
*Columnist/Pro Musician/Educator*

Born and raised in Brooklyn NY, Pasquale "Pat" Bianculli, studied classical guitar with Jerry Willard and Edgard Dana, at the Guitar Workshop in Oyster Bay, NY. He received his M. Mus. degree from the State University of New York at Stony Brook in 1981. The same year, he had the honor of performing for the legendary guitarist, Andres Segovia, in Granada, Spain. As a recitalist, he has been heard across the U.S., Canada, Europe and the Caribbean. In 1983, he made his New York solo debut at Weill Recital Hall at Carnegie Hall. Both he and his wife, flutist, Kathy McDonald, have shared music teaching careers, and continue to consult as well as record and perform their own works.

**www.fluteandguitarduo.com**

### JESSE IAN HOPKINS
*Columnist/Luthier*

A 1998 graduate of the Galloup School of Lutherie, Jesse has worked as a repair technician for a number of local music stores in the Detroit, MI area. He also built guitars for Reverend Musical Instruments from 2000 to 2006 before being hired as a custom luthier at First Act Inc's Studio For Artists in Boston, MA.

After returning to Michigan in 2007, Jesse built the first in a series of prototypes of what would become his own personal line of guitars. In 2010, with the help of his father Larry, J&L Guitar Company was formally launched and the resulting instruments are a marriage of classic aesthetics and modern design. These elements are brought together using traditional "by hand" building techniques and only the finest woods and hardware.

**www.jandlguitarcompany.com**

### ANDREW SCOTT
*Columnist/Luthier*

Luthier, Andrew Scott, the brainchild of Colorado based Blindworm Guitars, is on a lifelong quest is to improve sound, beauty and functionality, by exploring non-traditional methods and pushing boundaries. His unusual sonic masterpieces incorporate unique materials and sleek design with equal obsession over precision and tonal quality. Andrew's custom instruments are typically tailored for specific clients.

**blindwormguitars.com**

### ROD DEGEORGE
*Columnist/Pro Musician/Educator*

Rod DeGeorge is a guitar teacher, live performer and highly prolific session musician. He has written, recorded and produced commercial jingles and compositions for several national ad campaigns and other television projects. Rod has shared the stage with various well known musicians as a sideman. As a composer he has also released solo material, and was featured by Guitar Player Magazine, reviewing the title track of his Cosmic Playground instrumental album. As a teacher, Rod developed "Future of Music", an educational program which received praise and support from The United Way.

**www.degeorgemusic.com**

contributors

### DOUG RAPPOPORT (AKA *DougE Rapps*)
*Columnist/Pro Musician/Educator*

Doug Rappoport has played guitar professionally since age 15 and has been playing lead guitar, touring internationally and recording as a member of the legendary Edgar Winter Band, for 10+ years. Doug has also composed for television, does a variety of session work including movie trailers, national-primetime commercials, and also did a stint as music director and composer for local Los Angeles talk show favorite, "The John Kerwin Show." As a faculty member of Hollywood's Musician's Institute/GIT, Doug teaches Private Lessons and Open Counseling. He is currently recording a solo follow-up to his 2008 debut album, BIONIC.

www.dougrappoport.com

### RAÚL RODRIGUEZ
*Columnist/Luthier*

Raúl Rodriguez was born in Gijón a small town in the north of Spain. His father is a musician , so musical instruments and records where around and they caught his attention at early age. He studied music, guitar and bass, and after years of playing he developed an interest about guitar technology. He took woodworking courses, early music plucked instrument building courses, where he learned to build baroque guitar, vihuela and viola de gamba, and using books and videos he learned about guitar building and repair. During three years he worked at the Manuel Rodriguez workshop doing different processes on the buildindg of a classical and flamenco guitar. For a period of two years he has been collaborating with ISP magazine writing articles about different technical aspects of the guitar. Nowadays he is running his own guitar repair workshop, giving service to professional and amateur musicians.

www.rtgsur.com

### ANTOINE GEDROYC
*Columnist/Luthier*

Born in Paris, France in 1973 from a British father and a French Mother.
Antoine started building and restoring everything from solid bodies to basses, acoustic flat and arch tops, and exotic instruments. After working in guitar stores as a repairman, running several stores, working as a guitar Tech, road managers on tours and Festivals, working on guitar shows, he moved to Vancouver Canada then Copenhagen Denmark to open his own workshop. Specializing in Vintage restoration but also one off custom builds. Now living in Savannah GA for 3 years and working with vintage guitars and fine instruments.

### JIM KATH
*Columnist/Luthier*

James Kath of Kath Custom Guitars has been a guitar player for 40 years, and has been teaching for the past 30. After high school he apprenticed for a master luthier in New Jersey for five years. Since then Jim has repaired, customized and built lots of great instruments and has met many interesting people. He's traveled, lived and worked in many places in the United States as well as South America. "There are great players everywhere and they all need a luthier now and then." Jim currently lives in Santa Fe, New Mexico.

www.kathguitars.com

# content

06

046

082

026

040

# Editor's Notes

Wow! It's hard to believe that Issue 4 is finally here, but as the old cliché goes, "Time flies when you're having fun!"

So what the hell is "Mojo"? It's definitely one of those words open to interpretation. Mojo is used in many contexts to describe a person/place/thing that stands out above and beyond all the rest. Or maybe just a new beverage at Starbucks... But you get the drift.

To me, Mojo in the context of guitars, is simply something you can't hold, touch or see, yet you feel and hear its presence nonetheless. And only certain luthiers have that magic and know-how to bring it with each and every build.

So in this issue we dug deep to see what makes some very special builders tick. Luthiers Joe Knaggs, Balazs Pohazska and Chuck Thornton were our top picks in the realm of Mojo. As you will soon discover upon exploring this issue, they simply have it.

We were also fortunate enough to land an interview with "Mr. Ray Gun" himself, rocker & flamenco stylist Steve Stevens. Steve is one of those players who, in my opinion, can bring all the technical stuff out of his bag of tricks if he so pleases, but chooses to play according to what the song needs first and foremost for ultimate perfection. And that is a Mojo approach to guitar playing!

Finally, this month we have added a new regular feature called "The Photographers' Vault". I find photographers in this industry are largely ignored. We are so focused on the musician and the gear that we forget about another important person, the photographer! In a guitar magazine, the musician, the guitar, the gear... are the key artistic subject matter. There's also so much art in "the shot" and the photographer's vision. So, for anyone – luthiers, guitarists, readers in general who've ever wondered, "Wow! I wonder who shot that!"-- we're introducing some fellow guitar connoisseurs who are also artists and experts behind the lens.


See ya in 90 days

Kelcey Alonzo
Editor in Chief, Guitar Connoisseur


**Cover Artist**

Franklin Sandoval graduated with honors in Arts/Illustration from Altos de Chavon School of Design Studies in 1992-1994, and National School of Fine Arts in the Dominican Republic. He has participated in collective exhibitions and contests. Sandoval has also done magazine illustrations for the Spanish military, and various other picture books & editions. He works in different techniques from traditional to digital.

# Balazs Prohazska

# Balazs Prohaszka, Euro Jazz & Luthier

*By Raúl Rodríguez*

What would have happened if Torres and others before and after him didn't have the vision and willingness to improve the guitar as it was known in their era? Perhaps The Beatles would have written all their music using a lute, and Paco de Lucia a "vihuela de mano". The same vision and willingness is what makes people like Balazs Prohaszka move in a new direction. He started learning to build and repair lute, guitar and violin family instruments, but as soon as he could, he focused on guitars. And that's what made him travel from his hometown in Hungary to Ireland, to work for Lowden/Avalon guitars and, where he continues working in his own workshop.

Balazs shares his thoughts with us about contemporary lutherie, wood, finishing, setup and even guitar selection. Don't miss the opportunity to read about his circular shaped top guitar "Mickey Mouse". As previous builders have done, he will help us to better understand this craft, and to think about what a guitar really is... I mean a "Guitar", not a mass produced guitar shaped article that sounds similar to the real thing. The guitar world is full of myths, i.e., "this wood/finishing/nut material is better than this other or gives you more of that…" Listen to the guitar makers and the guitars! Luthiers work hard every day, and they don't want to be myth busters. They just want to make better sounding and playing guitars.

As I like to say, "Don´t look too much. Listen and feel instead. At the end you will know better which guitar is the best one for you."

*Balazs inlays*

**Guitar Connoisseur:** I read about your learning experience at a Hungarian school and working experience as a double bass builder and restorer. Did you know from the very beginning that you wanted to focus on guitars?

**Balazs Prohazska:** Yes, I started to learn musical instrument making with the intention to work with guitars exclusively. It all started with the love towards archtop guitars. There are not many guitar makers in Hungary, so I had to work with the violin family at the start of my career. I learnt a lot from it and I have full respect for this branch of luthery, but I have never lost focus. And this is how I ended up in Northern Ireland, in the pursuit to work full time on guitars.

**GC:** Old violin and lute makers were truly innovators for their time. Do you think that working with these instruments helped you to gain a better understanding of geometry?

**BP:** I do not think despite all the effort to mystify this matter, that proportion is applied to musical instruments, I rather think ergonomics and functionality determined proportions and geometry, and it was an organic evolution of musical instruments based on experient instead of some forced application of the divine golden ratio. But

yes, working with those instruments rose my fascination on how the ideal proportions were developed, and the importance of it; why the line of the upper or lower bout running that particular way-- and just a slight change would make it uncomfortable to play… how scale length and body dimensions are interlocked. Working with double basses though, where all sorts of proportions are used, taught me different approaches of how to bring the best results in sound and playability. I also think luthiers of this era are as much of innovators as our predecessors. We learned to use different materials and modern technology, we are still able to build historic instruments with lush baroque decoration, but also developed modern styles in ornamentation, alternative shapes and proportions, new bracing designs based sometimes on testing techniques available only in the last few decades.

**GC:** Were you also able to apply the different hand tools and techniques used for this type of instruments to guitar building?

**BP:** Yes, I still use some tools guitar makers usually do not, and use joint techniques sourced from restoration experience, but with alternative use. Or just sharpening my tools the way bow makers do for a particular timber. I've used even violin style neck joint in some cases, or

Balazs Prohazska

*Closeup of opposite page Inlays*

jointing a carved piece of ornamentation the same way as a sound post repair patch is fitted. Although I like to experiment with alternative bracing styles for archtop guitars, my techniques are quite traditional. But it is rather the precision and technicality brought from violin making and restoration.

GC: All this background surely influenced the way you approach guitar building but, how do you think it did?

BP: I am not sure. I think it gave me broader experience, getting acquainted with different ideas and concepts, some little secrets working in different workshops. I was actually shocked to hear when the groove inside the top, along the edge was patented. It was a sort of natural concept for me knowing some luthiers applied this concept long before, and I used it myself on my archtops. However my building is evolving too… It also put me in opposition with several concepts used today which are not approved by my experience. Maybe the most obvious influence is in my archtop building as I carve and graduate

my tops using traditional approach and techniques. The precision required in violin and bow making maybe influenced the level I accept in joints or just making inlays. But I am not sure if it is not in my nature regardless (of) this background. Currently I am experimenting to reintroduce hide-glue into my guitar making as you learn to appreciate its strength from violinmaking and repair…

GC: Are you still working for Avalon nowadays or are you just working at your own workshop?

BP: Currently I am still working on basically how to revive the brand. I still provide them with inlays and work on some other parts… like bevels on their guitars, but my primary focus is on my own instruments.

GC: Can you please tell us which are, in your opinion, the most obvious differences between a one man workshop and a bigger production one like Avalon?

BP: I can not call Avalon a bigger production line company as it is rather a custom shop setup. However I worked with several different sized companies in the Far East, but I guess it is a different matter again. It is easy to summarize: any production line lacks certain degree of attention to detail, and there is no individual approach to each guitar produced. I pick particular bracing material for particular tap tone or required sound. I have the flexibility to apply slight changes in bracing design if the overall design requires it. I think about each individual instrument as whole, how the materials work together and can be paired, what are my customer's requests. How can I produce harmony and balance? Such level of attention is impossible to achieve in any production line. But the main difference for me, we build a guitar with passion meanwhile a guitar in a production line remains only a guitar in a thousand…

GC: Do you build all kind of guitar family instruments (classical, flamenco, acoustic, etc.) or are you more focused on a particular one? Do you have a favorite? And why?

# Balazs Prohazska

*Balazs Prohazska at work*

BP: I have never built a Selmer style Jazz or a Flamenco. Also, I do not really wish to build electric guitars other than for my own pleasure, although I have built some electric basses. I am building classical guitars, steel-string flat tops and archtop guitars, and currently having some encounter with the mandolin family, so far a great success... Sometimes I wish I could focus on one or two particular models. Sometimes I enjoy the variety of instruments I have to build. I do not have a favorite. My favorite instrument is always the actual piece I am currently working on.

GC: Apart from bringing new concepts in guitar design, how do you approach top bracing? Do you make variations over a traditional layout or have you also develop your own?

BP: In most cases I use variations of traditional designs. I use basically x-bracing on steel strings, sometimes changing the angles or the relative position to the bridge, size, height, scallop, behind the bridge arrangement. But I have my own concepts too. For classicals, I use modified fan pattern, but also trying to involve more the upper bout so my design on the upper part of the body differs. As my building evolves I started to apply x-bracing concepts to the back, and also changing the back radius. This approach will be applied soon on all my flattop instruments. I either use parallel or x-bracing on my archtops, and unlike most of the builders these days, I prefer parallel bracing. I also used asymmetrical designs on archtops, which allowed me different "thicknessing". And I wish to continue experimenting with this.

GC: Do you experiment with bracing material?

BP: Not really. Most cases I use Sitka spruce. Occasionally European spruce, Lutz or Adirondack spruce. I am rather traditional in this regard, and I try to use only wood. I wish to try larch as bracing material as it is extremely stiff with superior sound conducting properties but so far I did not have a chance to try. I prefer to use European Lutz for archtop instruments.

GC: What do you think about the idea that the top is the most influential part of a guitar body in terms of tone, and the choice of the back and sides materials is not so important?

BP: I agree that the top mostly determines the tone. However one benefit working in a manufacturing environment is having the chance to widely experience the effect of different back and side materials on otherwise identically built guitars, using the same top, often from the

# Balazs Prohazska

**Balazs Prohazska's SJ African faces, inspired by Picasso**

Pictured: "La Madeline" Flamenco

# Balazs Prohazka

Belfast inspried Inlay

# Balazs Prohazka

# Balazs Prohazska Classical with Maple Scarf joint

Balazs Prohazka

# Balazs Prohazska

*Heart themed guitar*

same tree, neck and bracing. It definitely alters the characteristics of the sound and tone, can change the dynamics, balance, sustain and can even choke the sound even if the best top material is used, and weight and structure of the back has not been taken into consideration. As a result of this and personal experience, you will have your preferences, or you can choose better to contribute a particular sound. Also there are some combinations advised to avoid. Like using very hard, stiff Sitka with very dense materials- but it is up to the player and also the model size. Madagascar rosewood and ebonies will never become my favorite materials as a choice for back and sides despite their beauty. With some timber such Honduran mahogany, cocobolo, and recently Honduran rosewood, you would hardly get disappointed. Nevertheless you can achieve similar tone even using different top material with, and using appropriate back and sides or even neck materials. I believe you could even build a good sounding guitar from oak and rare grained pine if it is properly done. I haven't tried it though.

GC: The neck, fingerboard, the way it is built and attached to the body, and even fret material, are aspects that do strongly affect the final tone of a guitar. What do you think about this? Which materials and construction methods do you prefer?

BP: In most cases I use a dovetail neck joint. I am quite conservative in this regard. A wooden joint is a wooden joint. That is the beauty of our craft-- we work with wood using the highest level of precision and woodworking techniques, and a good dovetail is a wonderful example of these skills. I rather find the choice of neck material is rather important than the type of neck joint used. Honduran mahogany is a superior material, I rather do not like to use maple on flattop guitars, but sometimes some harder timber used in necks can improve sustain, responsiveness and add to the overtones... Nearly all my guitars have ebony fingerboard. I do not know any better to provide clarity and I rarely use alternative material. And if so, it is as dense as ebony and definitely heavier than rosewoods... The

fret material contributes only slightly to the sound along its size which also gives or takes away comfort in playing. I would prefer to use the hardest fret material, such as hard stainless steel or golden alloy fretwire, but I often compromise with this using more common harder nickel-silver fretwire, as this does not destroy all the tools in one setting.

GC: What's your favorite finishing material and technique? Why?

BP: My favorite finish is a good water based finish. It does not sink, looks natural, excellent to polish up to high gloss. Its drawbacks are: long drying times, laborious and can be tricky to spray. It can be applied thinly, and even though it dries to a hard finish somehow I found it very responsive. It is maybe the most similar to French polish, out of synthetic lacquers, but mainly I use high quality nitrocellulose; it is easy to work with, reliable and resilient, but being softer it needs more care. Also can be applied thinly, but often it sinks, and I use it for silky and not for high-gloss finishes. Alternatively, I

# Balazs Prohazka

can use French polish, it can bring up the beauty of the wood very well, but also can cause some patchiness on spruce or cedar. Unfortunately it is laborious.

GC: What design innovations have you made in order to improve ergonomics for the player?

BP: I designed several bevel styles for myself and for Avalon (I note Avalon is maybe one of the first applied bevels in a production line, including a back bevel long before others) including armrest bevels, also cutaway bevels. I can not call it my innovation as the basic concept is not mine although I have my approach and designed bevel styles no one else uses. My Mickey Mouse is an ergonomic victory with free access till the last fret. However, I rather find it fashionable styling than real ergonomic improvement using armrest bevels. Ok, maybe I have long enough arms not to feel any significant difference. I also use elevated fingerboards on my classical guitars, and along it changes the angle of the tension, it also gives more comfortable playing over the top.

GC: About your "Mickey Mouse', how did the idea of a guitar with a circular top start and develop? What did you want to achieve with this instrument? Can you please tell us about the materials and techniques used?

BP: As in most cases I find it hard to determine how an idea starts. Starts with some strange thoughts I suppose, or you just draw a shape think about the bracing, then change a little bit here and there if it feels better, till you reach a circle. But no, I had the circle concept as a definite starting point. After all, there are many circular concepts in the musical instrument world. I also did not want to disrupt it with a sound hole, so everything else was designed around it. I often get the impression the sound hole is simply in the way of designing a more effective and powerful bracing. And indeed all the instruments I built with offset sound holes sound superior. What I wanted to achieve is to prove there are other paths in guitar design, and you can bring the instrument to another level. Partly I succeeded, it sounds great and it is very comfortable to play. This design could be brought to crystallize the concept, but I have never expected it will be a business breakthrough. Still, whoever saw and played this instrument appreciated the craftsmanship involved and the quality on all levels even if it is a scary looking thing. Macassar ebony was used for back and sides, cedar top, Peruvian dark walnut multi-laminated neck with carbon fibre reinforcement, ebony bindings, bridge and soundhole ornaments.

GC: Why do you think that most of the builders and

players seem to prefer traditional concepts in design and materials rather than innovations? Can this be a matter of aesthetics or maybe a conservative aptitude?

BP: There are proven long established designs on the market. I understand if people trust something they got used to and it works well. But there is definitely a conservative attitude. After all, the common designs we use today were innovations once. I wish there would be more understanding what craftsmanship, and a particular concept exactly means and where it leads to and how it is executed. I also think it is lack of information that creates this situation, and it would be the responsibility of the luthier's community to provide information instead of some business minded propaganda that dominates our world, and in some cases is misleading.

GC: Lets talk about guitar setup. Of all adjustable parameters that are key to get a good playing action, intonation and tone, the nut is the one that seems to get less attention. What do you think about it? How do you

approach nut setup?

BP: I prefer the string slots running parallel as a continuation of the string, and not angled towards the tuners. The crucial factor for me is the bottom of the slot. The string should rest not only on the front edge of the slot but nearly the whole way leaving a small curved down and rounding apart at the rear end of the nut. So you have to find the proper angle while you are filing the string slot, making sure it leaves the nut at the very front and also rests in the slot well. I determine first, the place of the E strings measuring 3.5mm from the fingerboard edge, but it depends also the player and playing style and would be more on a classical guitar: 4-4.5mm. If I place a 6" ruler running from the slot (I have one with sharpened edge which guarantees it reaches the bottom of the slot), over the frets, I leave 0.1mm distance between the first fret and the ruler, but definitely not more than 0.2mm. I divide the distance between the outer string slots in a way that the distances between the strings are equal. I made a little tapered, slotted gauge for easy marking.

Finally, usually the high string plunges into the nut till the top of the string is on level with the top of the nut-- the bass side plunges half way. (ed note: "plunges" refers to how deeply the string sits in the nut slot, with the tops of high/unwound strings sitting level with the nut's top, while the top halves of the thicker low/wound strings are sitting above the nut.)

GC: Which do you prefer and why-- a neck nearly straight or one with some relief?

BP: It is up to the player really. If they prefer to play on a straight neck it is not a problem. Most people though are not even aware of any relief or straightness, and you sadly often encounter even professional musicians not knowing what is the use of the truss rod. My standard setup is with a small relief. On acoustic guitars I find it more controllable and easier if the neck moves forward under the string tension. There is a good chance the truss rod will not straighten it back perfectly, and then there is inconsistency, so I apply a small relief. Also on a steel string flattop

Balazs Prohazka

guitar with my top radius, it is a bit awkward to have a completely straight fingerboard without compromising with neck-angle and proper saddle height.

GC: Can you tell us about fingerboard and fretwork?

BP: Once again it really depends on the player. I always ask what fingerboard radius they prefer, if their preferred neck has a flatter or more cambered fingerboard. Not much news I could tell about fretting you would not find in any textbook. Crucial to have proper sized fret slots, or choose proper frets to avoid the frets deforming the fingerboard profile. All my fingerboards are bound, which means a little extra work, but then after it is the usual leveling, re-crowning process. I completely round the fret ends and polish up with very fine steel wool.

GC: If you where buying a guitar for yourself, what will be in your opinion the most important things to observe apart from aesthetics and tone/sound color?

BP: If I disregard the sound the first thing I check is the built quality: proper joints, proper neck angle and saddle height, proper setup, how refined the instrument inside, fretwork, how comfortable the neck is and overall construction. Looking for possible hidden faults (shockingly, like side-cracks even on higher-end guitars...). All this also determines playability. The second would be to check the quality of materials used.

GC: What is up for you in the near future?

BP: I am continuing building my own guitars, and that is what I enjoy most. I only wish I could find some time to build a few exhibition/experimental pieces. But I haven't even had time in the last few years to do so. Otherwise I have some consultation work in the Far East, and also working with several companies on a design level. I hope it will be business as usual. But I also need to free a few weekends finally for personal life...

www.prohaszkaguitars.com

# Cp Thornton Guitars

## Chuck Thornton-
### *Reinventing the Wheel*

**By Jesse Ian Hopkins of J & L Guitar Company**

When I was a young(er) luthier, I worked for guy who used to say "With guitar making, you have to sneak your innovations in quietly." This echoed something that I read in Bob Benedetto's book that where he wrote "Evolution is a slow process with the prolific makers at the helm". These sentiments seemed to cater to a mindset that thinks they just don't make 'em like they used to and a belief that if it isn't done the way Fender or Gibson did it, then it's not right. My experience building guitars at Reverend corroborated these statements as well as my budding notion that the general guitar playing public is just not ready for anything too forward thinking in terms of how their guitars are designed or built.

Thankfully, there are guys like Chuck Thornton, guys who have that sort of wide range, total-immersion-of-craft kind of experience. Guitar builders who have studied the past masters and absorbed all the lessons to their core, and whose guitars speak for themselves, but who aren't afraid to give you all the details. Luthiers who are, as a matter of fact, building them BETTER than "they" used to.

Damn, it's a good time to be a guitar player!

GC: You've got quite a storied history with the guitar. From studying at Berklee and giving private lessons, to building instruments with likes of Jon Cooper and Dana Bourgeois. Are there any one or two experiences/ lessons that most shaped your mindset or philosophy as it applies to your guitar making?

CPT: The guitar has been a part of my life since I was eight years old. I remember waking up morning after morning with my guitar on my bed because I played it before falling asleep, and would play it before I got out of bed.

As much as I love guitar, I've always wished I was a better player. So once I came to grips, after a year at Berklee, with the fact that I didn't have what it took to be a great guitarist, I didn't play as much as I once did.

Six or so years later when I started building guitars, and realized I had a talent for design, I started my second passionate journey with the instrument, focusing on trying to build the finest guitar I could possibly build.

When I went to work for Bourgeois guitars in 1993 I did a lot of repair work on the side, and time and time again would run into the same repair issues.

There was everything from ski jumps in the fingerboards, to broken headstocks, to poorly cut nuts, etc., and these issues were on expensive guitars.

I knew then that I didn't want to build a guitar in the same way it had been built just because that's the way it's been done for the past half century.

I wanted to address the areas of the instrument that I felt could be better.

GC: Has this mindset evolved over the years?

CPT: I'd like to think that I'm always evolving by designing new models and building my versions of existing models. For instance, I have a client who has 10 of my

# Cp Thornton Guitars

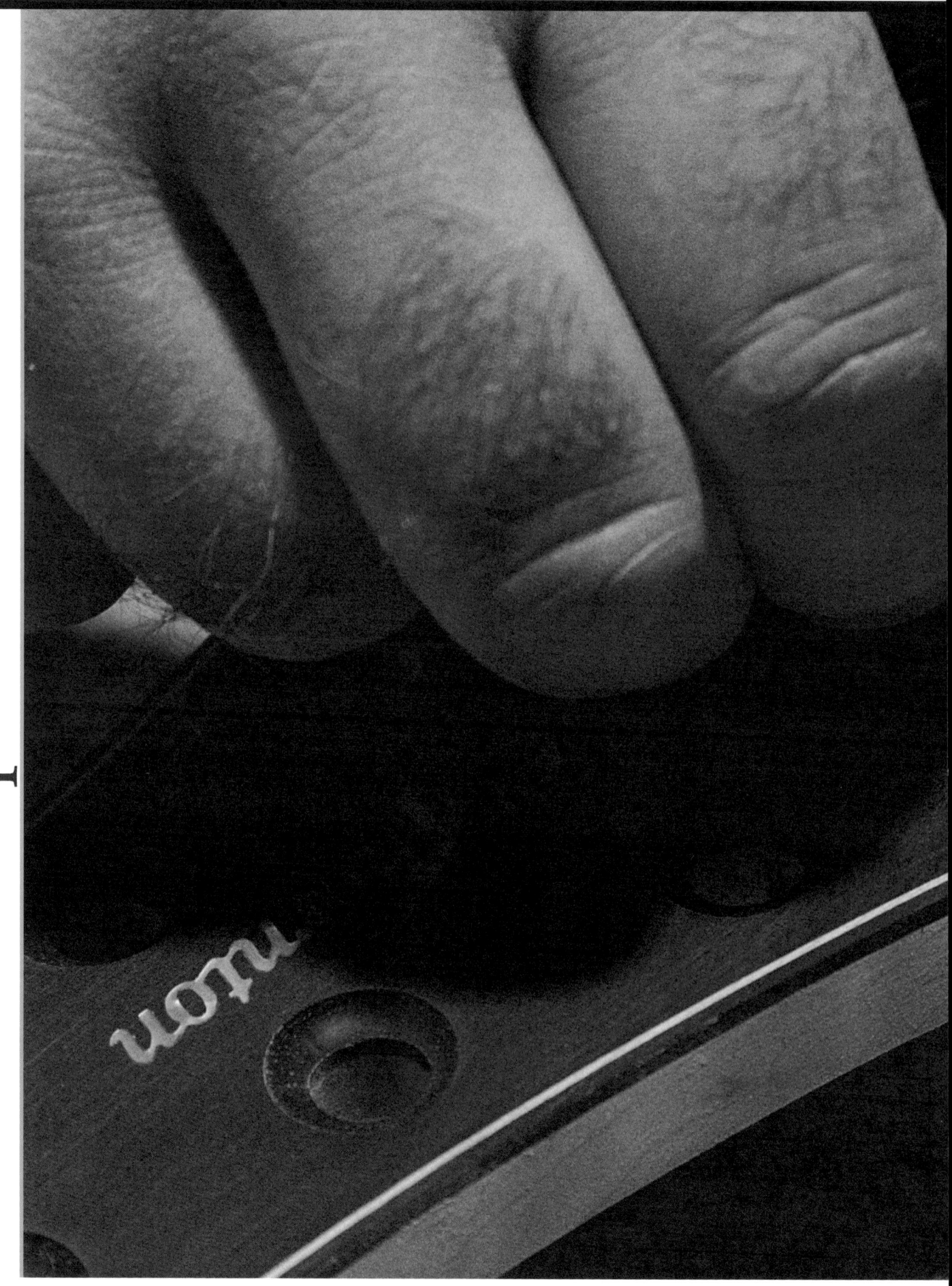

# Cp Thornton Guitars

*Chuck carving away*

guitars now, and wanted me to build him my version of two Gretsch styled guitars, so I'm building him my version of a Country Gentleman based on my "Improv", and a Penguin based on my "Blues Queen". These are not guitars I would have thought to do on my own but I'm very glad he has asked me to build them for him.

I don't want to ever become complacent with my guitars, I always want them to be the best they can be.

GC: Generally speaking, what makes a CP Thornton stand out? And are there any common identifiable qualities (sonic or otherwise) that all your guitars share?

CPT: I think what makes my guitars stand out is that they look familiar without strictly copying anyone else's designs. The two guitars that I build that come the closest to the original designs

are my Classic and my HTL, which stands for Homage To Leo. Not only is the profile slightly different than what you're used to, but the guitars also have a 4 degree neck angle instead of a negative neck angle like the originals.

My archtops, which include the Elite, Jazz Elite, Professional, Blues Queen, Professional Acoustic II, Improv and Acoustic Improv, are all carved from solid billets of wood, which are sonically different than a plywood top and back that are on most semi-hollowbody guitars.

But, because of my integral sound posts, along with the through neck design, the guitars don't feedback or have too bright a tone; they sing and sustain and, in my opinion, don't sound dead like a plywood top and back do.

GC: What is your most popular model and why? Do you have a personal favorite? If so, why?

*The inner workings of a 2006 Elite Jazz*

CPT: If you were an alto sax player or piano player or even a bass player, one great instrument would do the job.

What I love about the guitar is its extremely wide range of tones. Most of us aren't Clapton or Gilmour who can do most everything they do on one style of guitar. I think most of us want to learn the songs we grew up with and love, so if I want to play an Allman Bros. song I'm going to play it on one of my humbucker guitars. If I'm playing some Richie Blackmore I'll want my HTL withits single coils. I think this is what makes the electric guitar such a unique instrument and why so many of us have a lot of guitars.

I just built myself a semi-hollowbody Improv that I'm absolutely in love with. I've always wanted a good sized archtop, but not too big-- with fat tone, but without feedback. The semi-hollowbody Improv gives me everything I've ever wanted in this style of guitar.

GC: Do you offer anything in the way of custom building or do you stick to established models and options?

CPT: Some of my models were developed from custom orders. The Contoured Legend Special is a perfect example of that. One of my clients said that he's always wanted a Les Paul style guitar but didn't like the sharp edge on the top where his strumming hand rested, didn't like the weight of the guitar, and really loved the feel of a tummy tuck. So, I started with my Legend, gave it an arm slant and tummy tuck, and then dished out the back to make it lighter.

When I strapped the guitar on the first time, my initial reaction was not a lighter Les Paul style guitar, but more of a single cut SG style guitar. It's a very cool guitar that can be built as a 1 piece body out of some very exotic woods, like quilt mahogany, Tasmanian blackwood or koa.

GC: How many guitars do you typically produce in a year? Has your outputbeen affected by the current state of the economy?

CPT: I build three batches of guitars a year with 15 guitars per batch. Thanks to my incredible clients, most

# Cp Thornton Guitars

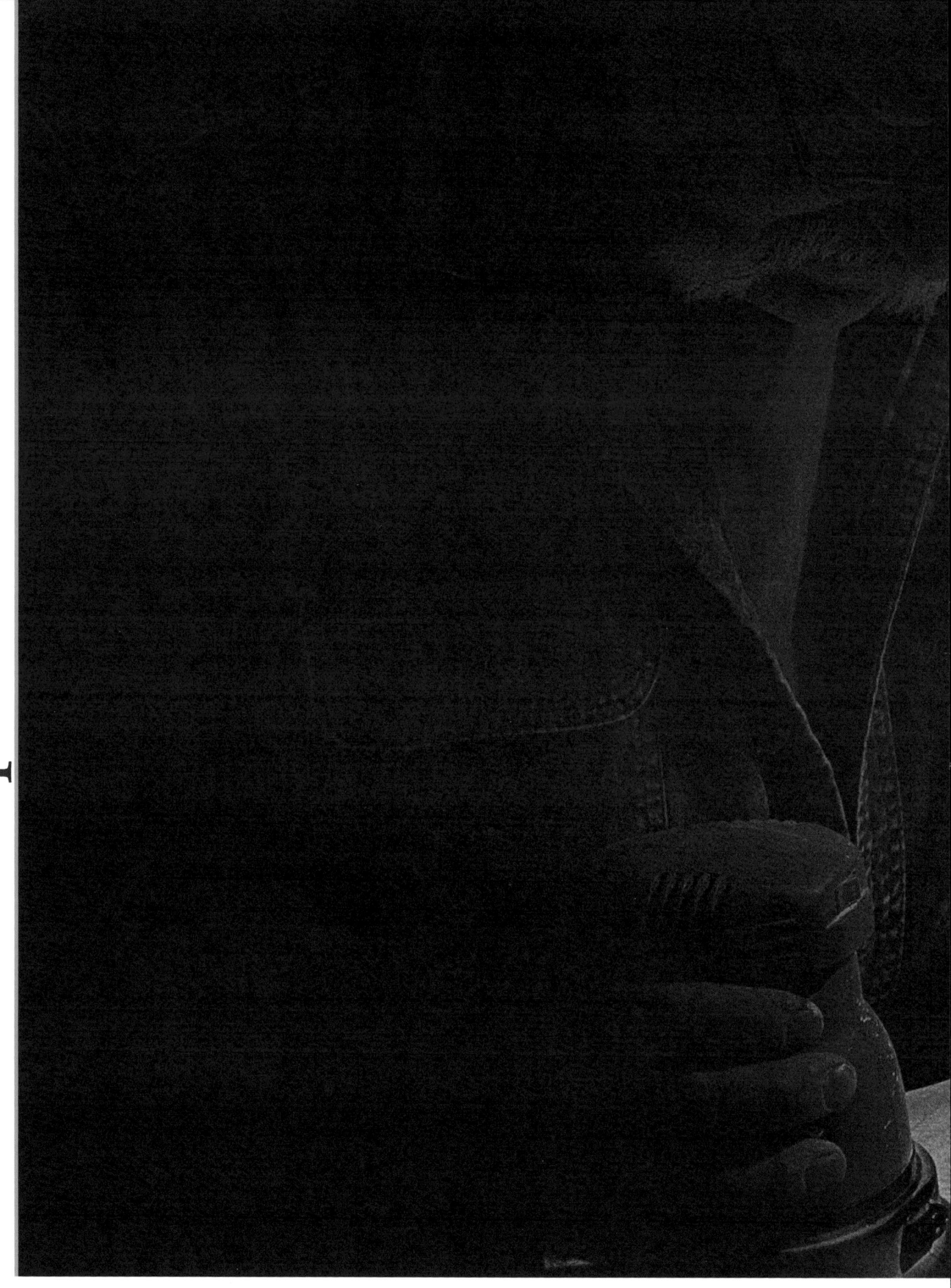

# Cp Thornton Guitars

of whom have become good friends, I have not felt the recession at all. I have one friend who has purchased 29 of my guitars to date, another friend who has I think 14 now with 4 more on order.

Another person who I have not met, but consider a friend, purchased 9 in one year! And another friend who I have not met has I think ten now and two on order in every batch this year. One way the economy has hurt me is one of my friend's, who purchased 13 of my guitars, business has been affected by this recession, and hasn't been able to buy any guitars in some time. I miss building guitars for him, and wish I could afford to build one for him and just give it to him.

GC: There seems to be an explosion of awareness and accessibility of boutique guitar makers, and talented new builders seem to be emerging allthe time. Where do you see this industry headed in the next 25 years?

CPT: This is without a doubt the best time in history to be a guitar player.

Even as recently as twenty years ago, it was pretty much unheard of for someone to buy a guitar without playing and hearing it first, and I think the reason for that was because you could play a dozen guitars before you found one that felt right or sounded great. I think guitar players are far more sophisticated now and are getting away from the big box store mentality of guitar making.

If you have four or five thousand of your hard earned dollars to spend, do you want to go into some big store and hope you can get what you want by picking it off the wall knowing, 1) - how many people worked on this guitar when it was built, and if they were having a good day or pissed off at the world, and took it out on the guitar, and 2) - how many people played the guitar before you got there and rejected it for one reason or another? Or would you rather talk to the person who's building your guitar, with his name on the headstock and his reputation on the line?

I think you'll see over the next 25 years the independent luthier taking more share of the market away from the big companies.

# Cp Thornton Guitars

Chuck Thornton-The Improv Model

# Cp Thornton Guitars

*Chuck taking a guitar through it's paces before it leaves the shop*

GC: What do you feel are your greatest/most innovative contributions to the guitar?

CPT: My carved radiused headstock is one. After seeing numerous broken headstocks I felt it was important to address this area. I carve a radius in the top of the headstock and a volute in the back of the headstock to get opposing radii. There's a lot of strength in a radius, so my thinking was to have two radii back to back so whichever way a guitar fell, hopefully there would be enough strength there to prevent a fracture. Three clients that I know of have dropped their guitars-- one so hard it broke the 5th string tuner off the guitar. But none of the headstocks have broken.

The through-neck design in my archtops is another feature that I'm very pleased with. With the traditional design you have an end block and a neck block that the neck is glued into, so over time with the weight of the strings pulling the tailpiece, pushing down on the bridge and pulling on the neck can result in a distorted or cracked top and, as it's been referred to, a "ski jump" in the fingerboard.

With the through-neck design, the neck is the end block and neck block, so now with the tension of the strings you don't get two blocks trying to pull towards each other, which cause ski jumps in the fingerboards and cracks in the top. I can't tell you how many times I've seen semi-hollowbodied guitars that fretted out past the 12th fret from this problem.

Another thing I do is, instead of bracing a top to withstand the pressure of the strings, I carve integral sound posts into the top and back, kind of like the sound posts a violin or cello would

have, only I do two sound posts under the bridge that get glued to the through-neck. And the sound posts from the back also get glued to the neck. I believe that these sound posts transfer energy from the bridge into the neck and back, and also stop any top distortion from the pressure of the strings. They also dampen the top which I believe reduces feedback.

Another thing I do to solve the feedback issue in a semi-hollowbody, is that the pickups are in their own pockets instead of hanging inside an open box, which can cause microphonic feedback.

GC: Have you achieved what you set out to do with CP Thornton Guitars, and what legacy do you hope to leave behind?

CPT: What I set out to do was to build the finest guitar I could possibly build. So as long as I'm alive, that's what I strive to do.

When I worked for the violin maker (Jon Cooper) there were times he would sit and study an old violin for hours, studying the workmanship, the graduations in the top or the bee-sting in the purfling on an instrument that was two hundred plus years old, and worth so much more than the maker ever would have dreamed his work could be worth. I hope for the same with my guitars, and I hope the same for the people who have purchased my guitars, that they become more valuable than anyone would have ever dreamed.

# Namm 2013

Photo Credit: Mike Ingram

Rocky Junior Special

## the NAMM show[13]

by JP Holesworth

How do we begin a concise review of our Winter NAMM experience in Anaheim?

Hmm… Well, first of all I wasn't planning on attending at all. And Gc's Chief Editor, Kelcey wasn't about to leave the East Coast as his wife was due with a baby in late January (btw, a baby girl was born Jan. 25th — and the show ran 1/24 – 1/27. They shoulda named her Nammitha). Another setback, LA guitarist & Gc contributor Doug Rappoport would end up not attending due to a bout with the flu. We did have LA based Pentatonic Productions set up to represent us at NAMM for some film features with Eric Gales, Fibenare Guitars and C.F. Martin & Co. Otherwise, the core Connoisseur crew wouldn't be attending.

Then at the last minute, I had an opportunity to go, at the invitation of some very generous gear industry folks who needed a NAMM networking presence. I also represent my blog stratoblogster.com, but fortunately had a NAMM media badge for Gc. People confuse Guitar Connoisseur with Guitar Aficionado all the time, which is on not necessarily a bad thing in our stage of infancy.

*Fibenare Guitars unveiled the "Fibenare-Sin" Guitar; a collaborative effort with hungarian artist Oliver Sin*

Flying into LAX from the Pacific NW, I was ready for some sunshine— though Anaheim ended up being cloudy and rainy every morning. Still it was balmier than back home in Washington State. For much of the show I would be accompanied by a veteran gear industry consultant, responsible for assisting the finance of this trek, to whom I will refer as "my attorney".

**Dave Mustaine showing off his Double Neck Dean**

The day before the official show start-up, I was able to catch NAMM 's Media Event. This was a micro version of NAMM with a cross section of selected vendors in mini booths, plus a press conference area and COOKIES! Andy Powers of Taylor Guitars was on hand introducing their newest Grand Orchestra body style models, designed by Andy, an accomplished boutique builder before joining Taylor as top designer. It was great speaking with Andy about the process of building a new model from the ground up, the old fashion way, before adapting for larger scale production.

**TC Electronic** was promoting their new "Ditto" looping pedal. In a tiny housing, this very simple delay is for on-the-fly use. TC's demonstrator did everything I would want from a looper, without a bunch of tap dancing and quantizing, whatever that means… See, my Digitech JamMan Solo gathering dust cuz I need martial arts, fighter pilot training to figure it out.

As I was grazing the cookies, Dean Guitars introduced Megadeath's Dave Mustaine at the nearby press podium, to introduce his newest double neck V signature guitar, and say a few thank you's. The oatmeal raisin cookies were mega-good! Also about this time I ran into Peter Hodgson of I Heart Guitar blog, who freelances for several guitar publications. Peter arrived from

Australia a few days earlier to visit Disneyland and Seymour Duncan headquarters; not a bad way to prime oneself for NAMM. It was great to finally meet someone I've networked with online for a few years. Next, I was watching an impromptu jam in the aisle from guitarist Alex Skolnick and a serious Jazz trumpet player. You run into many of these throughout the show.

That evening I was able to get into Fender's Private Event, thanks to my attorney. Of course we made a beeline for the Custom Shop area where plenty of serious Masterbuild instruments were already heavily tagged for the NAMM Special dealer drawings they do. The focal bling display of the year was a diamond studded Tele/Cabronita build by Yuri Shishkov marked at $120K. The John Cruz & Dale Wilson guitars stood out as well. Fender's vast area also includes Gretsch, Guild & the EVH line. I didn't catch Eddie himself, but there was an adequately trained clone on hand demoing all the trademark acrobatics with the latest EVH gear,

*Paulino Bernabe Booth*

sans Marlboros and soul. The food was okay, though I expected better fare from Fender (I was starving at the time). I really dug the Gretsch displays with the Bo Diddley, Billy Bo and Chet Atkins guitars. Topping things off was Greg Koch demoing the new '57 Bandmaster tweed RI. Koch has amazing chops and tone; some of the best I'd witness over the entire NAMM visit.

Wisely, in preparation of the opening day, I installed the invaluable NAMM smartphone app, grabbed a hardcopy map, and put together an itinerary mostly based on Hall/Booth numbers. There are several convention halls, so it's not enough to know booth numbers alone. Planning by halls is essential, even though European attendees don't hesitate letting you know that Musikmesse in Frankfurt is "many times" larger than NAMM… Replay that previous phrase in a German accent-- as if to say, "NAMM is your wimpy American copy of Musikmesse!" And more recently I heard about a gear show in China that's supposedly even more massive than Musikmesse. Holy cow!

*Titanium Guitars by Bad Seed*

To me, NAMM is expansive enough ALREADY-- especially if you wanna see ukuleles, the current "fad" instrument. I started in Hall E with a plan to work my way backwards to Hall A, plus minor trips to other areas called "Levels" which are dominated by larger companies like Gibson & Fender. Oh, and The Marriott across the street from Anaheim Convention Center was pretty much owned by Yamaha, so that was another adventure.

Hall E is one of my favorites because it's quite diverse with smaller and newer vendors. Hall E was also home to easily over a dozen Ukulele booths, big booth areas too! You see, ukuleles are popular these days, like Justin Bieber. They're a cute little instrument that gives the world its sugar rush of the moment. So of course, large Asian manufacturers of toys, housewares, gardening tools, adult novelties, etc., have suddenly tooled up for uke production. And all the ukes on earth were in Hall E (or at least I thought so, until I got to Hall D). Let's just say most of

*Trussart Reverse Brass Top*

them were in E, okay.

Actually, just so you know, most of the boutique guitar makers on my itinerary ended up being in Hall C. But like I said "E" is interesting. Minarik had a large display of their ever mystical shaped guitars. And speaking of mystical & metaphysical, I met the folks from Colorado-based **Crystal Frets** who will re-fret your guitar with quartz crystal which they say will never wear out, for under $1000. That stuff is legal in Colorado now. **Caparison Guitars** was a must stop, but oddly and sadly there was no **Eklundh** Apple Horn signature model on display—and no Mattias IA Eklundh in sight, so I kept movin'. Australia's **O'Donnell Custom Guitars** was there with 3 beautiful electrics. That's a one-man operation, so ya gotta respect a guy who travels so far alone with 3 guitars, especially on United or Delta. No surprise, **Tom Anderson** Guitarworks had more flame & curly maple tops on display than anyone. Also in Hall E, we visited **AudioFly**, makers of an innovative new in-ear monitor product that doesn't look like those big, bulky things you see on stage most of the time. I met with Kevin at J. **Backlund Design Guitars** who make these cool "retro-future" solidbody guitars that remind me of 50's Corvettes & T-Birds, as well as The Jetsons cartoon. Be sure to visit their link! **Peekamoose Guitars** has a line of bolt neck guitars with some crazy burst finish combos. This booth was run by a couple of real young cats who said the company was named after a ski resort in Upstate NY.

And more ukulele booths.

*Eric Gales at the Two-Rock Booth*

The list of interesting booths at Hall E alone was endless. Other noteworthy booths in E included, **Heritage, Collings** and a nifty little Louisiana based outfit called **Baudier Guitars.** Acoustic makers **Santa Cruz, Lowden** and **Breedlove** displayed beautiful hi-end instruments. Equally impressive were the works of Spanish classical builders **Paulino Bernabe** and **Admira.** Who could cover it all!

By the way, it's good to keep yourself hydrated at NAMM. On my attorney's advice I picked up a case of bottled water at a nearby Target and set out each day with 4 bottles in my laptop case while the laptop lived at the hotel. Unfortunately, I didn't bring the shoulder strap, which made urinal trips tricky as ya don't wanna set it down just anywhere, much less in a splash zone. So I'd be holding the case on my head with one hand… And button fly jeans too! Moving right along.

HALL- D is a train wreck because most of the planet's drum companies are located here. I guess the "D" for drums makes it simpler for drum society to navigate at NAMM. Unfortunately, non-percussion vendor booths get interspersed within drum city, and it can be deafening in some areas. Again, the Euro folks will tell you that Musikmesse handles the drum situation much better. Otherwise, some of my favorite exhibitors were in this hall.

**Aristides Instruments** of the Netherlands were debuting their O2O model, a slightly toned down instrument from the sports car looking O1O Adrian Vandenberg guitar. These guitars are made from a ceramic glass composite material they call "Arium". I wanted to check out a chunk, but I guess it can't leave Amsterdam in "chunks"… too many questions. Real nice fellas though!

I met Steve Carr and Dave Quick of **Carr Amps.** Crafty little combo amps! Besides the boutique/retro looks, Carr really knows amp building for tone! Their test guitar was an old beater Tele Nashville config autographed by Danny Gatton, Bill Kirchen and Link Wray. What's better than that!

**Premier Builders Guild** was sadly stuck in the worst part of the drum zone. PBG is a group of outfits i.e. **Gene Baker, Koll, Fano, Giffin** and **Two-Rock Amps.** They're also involved with the current line of D'Angelico archtops displayed just across the aisle. This was the site of the **Eric Gales** jam filmed on Friday that included 12 year old phenom Ray Goren. I was able to briefly meet Gales just before that performance, and got a good close view of the jam between the two guitarists and 40 drummers. Our video includes interview segments shot right after, at the hotel.

New Zealand based **Bad Seed Custom Guitars** had an array of crazy metal guitars; many titanium, in standard profiles, i.e. S-type,

T-type, single cut and even an Explorer. Sheldon, the founder digs making stuff out of titanium including pickup covers and other hardware. These guitars sound and feel really good, and have plenty of traditional vibe with edginess where needed. I wouldn't mention them if they were simply nerdy. Cool stuff, so check them out!

TonePros Production Mgr, Gil Vasquez is launching **Vane Guitars**, and had some classic sporty lookin' prototypes featured at the TonePros booth. Gil is a gear industry veteran who has worked with Parker Guitars and a few others in the production mgmt capacity. Keep an eye out for the Vane line!

**Perri Ink Guitars** aka Perri Ink Cartel was my personal favorite of Hall D. Nick & wife, Misi Perri, run an LA based custom guitar shop where they also build custom motorcycles—and you can get tattoos there as well. Sounds random, but these kids put their brand continuity into everything they touch. The booth had rusty chain link fence walls and a work bench complete with a big honkin' bench vise and a tore down V twin engine. The guitars are T & S-types with hi-end parts, finishes and set ups. Fun!

Hall C was quieter! Ok, just know that nowhere at NAMM is quiet. But just stepping out of Hall D into the commons area was nearly a spiritual transformation. I almost expected Morgan Freeman to appear at my side in a white suit for a calm and comforting chat. And speaking of metaphysical, Carvin had their Allan Holdsworth signature model display right along the main aisle, backed by a glaring life size photo of Allan who seems to warn you not to touch the guitar. As I walked past the display, his eyes followed me. Even when I did a u-turn they continued following me. That was my Carvin experience. Not on the itinerary.

Two of our favorite German builders, **Ritter Instruments** and **Nik Huber** Guitars shared a substantial booth space in Hall C. Both have been featured here at Gc, so be sure to see links to their interviews and pictorials in our back issue archive on the back page. Jens Ritter is a fun loving cat who builds over-the-top basses and guitars. Seeing some of these in person is awe inspiring. Nik Huber was constantly busy, so we never had a chance to meet. When these guys are working with people who have their credit cards out, it's best to give 'em plenty of space! And Huber's inspirational guitars were getting serious attention.

**James Trussart** Custom Guitars has an ever growing line extending well beyond their familiar distressed steel T-types to several profiles with wood bodies, brass tops and hollow reso-types as well. France based Vigier Guitars, known for their Shawn Lane models, brought several very progressive instruments this year including a fretless S-type with a stainless steel fingerboard.

Somewhere in the middle of all this, not even sure which hall, I walked into an amazing booth performance by bass god Jeff Berlin. The booth belonged to a company that puts multi-color coatings on bass strings. Sorry I've forgotten who they are. Suddenly & unexpectedly standing a few feet from Berlin and his mighty chops was certainly a high point of my NAMM experience!
BTW, there's a "Black Sabbath for Ukulele" book. Not kidding!

Hungarian luthiers **Fibenare Guitars** (see video), had some of the finest electric guitars of the show. These folks are really about hand crafting, as they even make hardware and pickups with wooden mounting rings. Real sexy too! I was honored to test drive their Roadmaster '56 T-type

*Jens Ritter at Namm 13'*

*Mike Lipe of Lipe guitars*

which is a work of art in every way! No, that's not me in the video… I wish I could play like Tom Quayle. And speaking of art work, Fibenare also displayed a canvas by noted Euro painter **Oliver Sin**; complete with a matching guitar painted by Sin. Pretty high brow stuff… But even more classy, they offered me a beer! Before the end of the Cold War, these cats were building their own guitars as kids; making frets out of bicycle spokes. So God bless 'em, and the road they've travelled.

Hall B was a must for me, if only to check out **LSL Instruments** who build a Carl Verheyen signature model S-type. LSL produces a very unpretentious and arguably underpriced line of standard profile guitars. These guitars are made with love, for players by Lance Lerman and crew in Southern, CA. Their sugar pine body T-types weigh down to nearly 4 lbs, and LSL makes their own rounded edge bolt necks and pickups. Instead of serial numbers, each guitar has a sticker with a different female name on the neckplate. When I asked Lance why a sticker instead of stamping or engraving the plates, he quickly responded, "Have ya ever been through a divorce?" Pretty laid back bunch. Sweet guitars!

I spent some time at **CF Martin** in Hall B, where the film crew would be doing a profile later on. Everyone knows Martin. They're still family owned, and had a huge space full of the kinds of guitars they've been cranking out for generations. You just want to stand in the middle and meditate in the Martindom of it all. OM!!! The video reveals some of the latest things Martin is up to.

**Moses Graphite** was interesting. We hung there a bit, checking out their graphite replacement necks for F-type guitars. If you're not familiar with Moses, please visit them online.

Although the show ran Thursday thru Sunday, my attorney advised that we needed to leave Saturday AM. So I had to stick to a tight itinerary—meaning, lots of exhibitors I can't focus on. Besides, this piece has to have an end anyway, right? I'm getting there, alright. Hall A was a blur…

Friday evening, I wrapped up NAMM with a visit to **Gibson**. Like Martin, Gibson spans over a century of American instrument making. And in spite of all the changes, Gibson's space was loaded with history and lots of beautiful guitars… LOTS of 'em! I was fortunate to be introduced to Don Ruffatto who helps run the Bozeman, Montana facility, where Gibson's hi-end acoustic guitars are produced. Montana's dry climate provides the key environmental conditions for building stable acoustics. A fan of small bodies (just not ukuleles), I gravitated right to the Keb Mo signature model, an L series Blues box.

Also at Gibson, I really enjoyed some time with Mike Voltz of the Memphis Division. Mike has been with Gibson since the Kalamazoo days, and is pretty much the go-to authority on Gibson's electric history. A close friend of Elvis' guitarist Scotty Moore, Mike showed us Scotty's gold ES-295, along with a small Magnatone combo amp that has spent most of its life in the Moore family kitchen. Mike has plenty of Scotty & Elvis stories, plus he let us handle some awesome Custom Shop VOS ES-330's, 335's and Les Pauls. I was afraid to even touch the large, shiny new archtop models.

Sadly, I had to end my NAMM experience early with nearly a third of the show yet unexplored to my satisfaction. Hall A was a quick walk-thru. Perhaps the biggest personal item I missed was trying to catch David Grissom at the PRS booth. But for Guitar Connoisseur purposes, it was great to focus on boutique as much as possible. Certainly, there were many more booths to visit, and ukulele exhibits to dodge. Hopefully next time, with more days available, and 2-3 Gc stooges attending, we'll get an even better view. Not bad for our first NAMM!

Final note: Besides all that NAMM stuff, I truly enjoyed the Rocco Red Ale by Bootlegger's Brewery—on tap at Clancy's, on Harbor Blvd. My attorney concurred.

*Fender custom shop*

# Joe Knaggs

GLOVE FACTORY, Greensboro, Md.

How many guitar builders would leave a top executive/creative position with one of the largest guitar companies, after over 20 years, to start over from scratch with their own company? That's what Joe Knaggs did, after being with PRS since 1985, but bidding farewell in order to found Knaggs Guitars in 2010.

The creator of PRS's Private Stock instruments, Joe was as much at the top of PRS as anyone could be without being Paul Reed Smith himself. The only thing that remained was being able to put "Knaggs" on the headstock.

Joined by former PRS Sales & Marketing Director, Peter Wolf, Knaggs and a small, tight crew are setting new standards for American boutique guitars on par with what we're seeing in fine craft instruments from Germany, Belgium and Finland these days, while all too many US "builders" continue to bolt together after market bodies and necks with hot rod paint jobs.

The Knaggs guitar line combines technical innovation and craftsmanship with top materials and just enough familiarity to avoid scaring away a typically conservative guitar market. Instruments include both solid and hollow

Hand Colored

body electrics, basses and a series of flat-top acoustics. Models are currently categorized in 3 easy to understand "Tiers"; Tier 1 being the top price/features point. Although Joe's experience and industry savvy is certainly an advantage, remember he has had to muster fresh ingenuity to reinvent and replace a number of approaches and tech designs that had to remain at the previous gig... as well as reinvent himself. He also has to make sure the new place has coffee, stamps, paperclips and TP!

Most of us would have chilled it at PRS with a little fishin' on the side and a nice retirement on the horizon. But we're not Joe Knaggs, who is naming his guitar models after North American rivers. Even the "Choptank"—look it up!

Guitar Connoisseur is very proud to bring you the following interview with a true leader in the new wave of American luthiers!

# Joe Knaggs

Photo Credit: Michael G Stewart

*Joe Conceptual Abstract*

GC: We know you're on good terms with PRS, and have many friendships there. Do you still get many calls for help and advice from those who replaced you?

JK: First of all. Thank you so much for the kind words ! This really means the world to myself and all the rest of us here at Knaggs Guitars !

I do have many friends at PRS still. There are people there that I spent 25 years with. Although, I do still see, and talk to people from PRS, I do not get many request s for help. We have conversations around life outside of work, which is what I prefer. There are guys like Matt Eriza that are like a brother to me. I would much rather talk about soccer w/ him. On the other hand, if friends from PRS, including Paul would ask for help, I would help them anyway I could….

GC: I saw in another interview that you are (or were) exporting more guitars than are sold in the US. Is this still the case?

JK: It is beginning to even up… Our first relationships were with Sound Service of Germany, Ishibashi of Japan, and Zoom from England. Peter's relationship with Jorchen ( the owner of Sound Service) is what got the ball rolling there, and my name was very well known in Japan. Peter and I spent quite a bit of time growing the Private Stock program there, so Ishibashi approached us. My name as a high end luthier was well known overseas, but also in the U.S. with individual dealers and end use customers…

I believe the U.S. dealers would have got on board with Knaggs Guitars quicker if they did not have such stock in their stores… Many of them did not need any more high end product, especially a product which could possibly conflict with their other relationships. PRS in particular… That is starting to change, and will most likely take a bit more time…The economy having a major role in all of it. The end use customers, and a dealer bought ,and put half down on the original serial number 1 guitars. This was a major key to starting the business, as we did it all on a shoe string. Thanks guys !

GC: Not to assume because of the current economy, because you obviously didn't strike out on your own at the best time either… do you happen to sell more Tier 1 models regardless?

Photo Credit: Larry Melton

Severn T2 Chocolate Creme

Joe Knaggs

Severn T2 Ocean Blue

# Joe Knaggs

Photo Credit: **Markus Kaes**

*Kenai Headstocks getting finished up*

JK: We sell a very even mix of T1, T2 and T3 product…. I believe we will sell more T1 product in the future, and I am beginning to build some super high end "one off" instruments that we will name "The Creation Series". My passion is to create! I/we will be creating individual works of art, much like "one off" original paintings. Of course they will play and sound great as THAT is the goal !

GC: Your instruments are all named after North American rivers, including the "Choptank" (I checked). What influenced this, are you a fisherman when time allows?

JK: I am not really a Fisherman, although I love it, and landed a 12 ft. Marlin one time…

I spent much time in nature. I love being outdoors and one of my favorite things in my life is the time I spent near waterfalls and rivers. I backpacked and camped continuously as a kid, and we would always make sure that our destination for the night was a river. I love the sound that water makes flowing over rocks, the power it has, the peace it has, and the fact that a trickle at the top of a mountain ends up in the vastness of the seas.

My original concept of the brand was to name it

"Chesapeake", and have all the models named after the tributaries of the Chesapeake Bay.. That is where Choptank, Severn, Patuxent, and Potomac came from…

Markus, our dear friend, which handles the website, advertising layouts, etc…. suggested naming it "Knaggs". He felt that the name had a uniqueness about it, which would stick in peoples mind. Plus, people want to have the luthier's name on their product. Peter and I both agreed with this concept. So, under "Knaggs Guitars", there is the "Chesapeake Series", and the "Influence Series"…
We wanted there to be a clear line between the different series, so we decided to name the Influence series after North American rivers in general, and… quite frankly, the Indian named rivers had the best sound… I also have always had a love for the "spirit" of the "American Indians". Peter and many other Europeans also have a fascination with American Indians because of American history, and films…

GC: Has it been a challenge having to re-design various components to replace ideas you had to leave behind at PRS? Or are you good at cranking out alternate solutions and workarounds?

*Kenai T2 Hickory Burst*

JK: Many of the reasons I/we started the company was to utilize and present these concepts I had in the shapes, and hardware. I do not know if I am good at "cranking out" alternatives, but the ideas I had were certainly not "workarounds". Although we agree on many things that make a great guitar, I have a very different concept of what a guitar should sound like than Paul has... or maybe better stated , "than what I personally like in the sound of a guitar".

The laminations, body shapes, and most of all- bridge designs were something that I had been conceiving in my mind for 10 years.
I wanted bridge designs that transferred the energy/sound into the body as much as possible. All three bridges ( hardtail, trem and influence ) do this by linking the original point of contact ( string holding), with the down pressure point (break across the saddle) into the body.

The bridge plates are solidly held down, so that everything else can transmit without wasted vibration. I have designed the trem bridge to use a hinge type approach, rather than a "knife edge" approach. The front plate of the trem bridge is screwed down solid into the body... This way you can use softer woods like swamp ash or quilt maple, and the screws won't work their way loose or get "sloppy" as will happen with a "knife edge".

We have a unique sound in our guitars. They have very clear deep bass, full low midrange, and very round highs. The guitars do not carry a lot of "high midrange". That has never been a favorite harmonic range of mine as it tends to sound "nasily", but to each his own.

For some reason, I do not mind more high mid range in acoustics....

GC: Does the Influence Series tailpiece to bridge interface also address tightness of the tune-o-matic on the posts like TonePros does with their set screw approach?

JK: The main thing the Infuence tailpiece does is solidify the post into the body through the brass plate. The posts are screwed into the brass plate first and then into the body. I like the thinner posts, and this helps strengthen them... I have seen guitars that have such high neck angles the thin posts are bending.

The other key factor is the bridge plate links the string holder with the break point of the saddle as I described in the last question.. This drives all that sound into the body as one bridge...

GC: Tell us about the "hinged" trem design on the Severn (S-type)-- does the T-style bridge pickup plate act as the mass to hinge with?

JK: Yes, that is correct... It strengthens, but also gives the guitar the T- style sound w/ a normal single coil pickup as the pickup is

# Joe Knaggs

Photo Credit: Peter Wolf

Photo Credit: Peter Wolf

# Joe Knaggs

**Sheyenne T2 Ocean Blue**

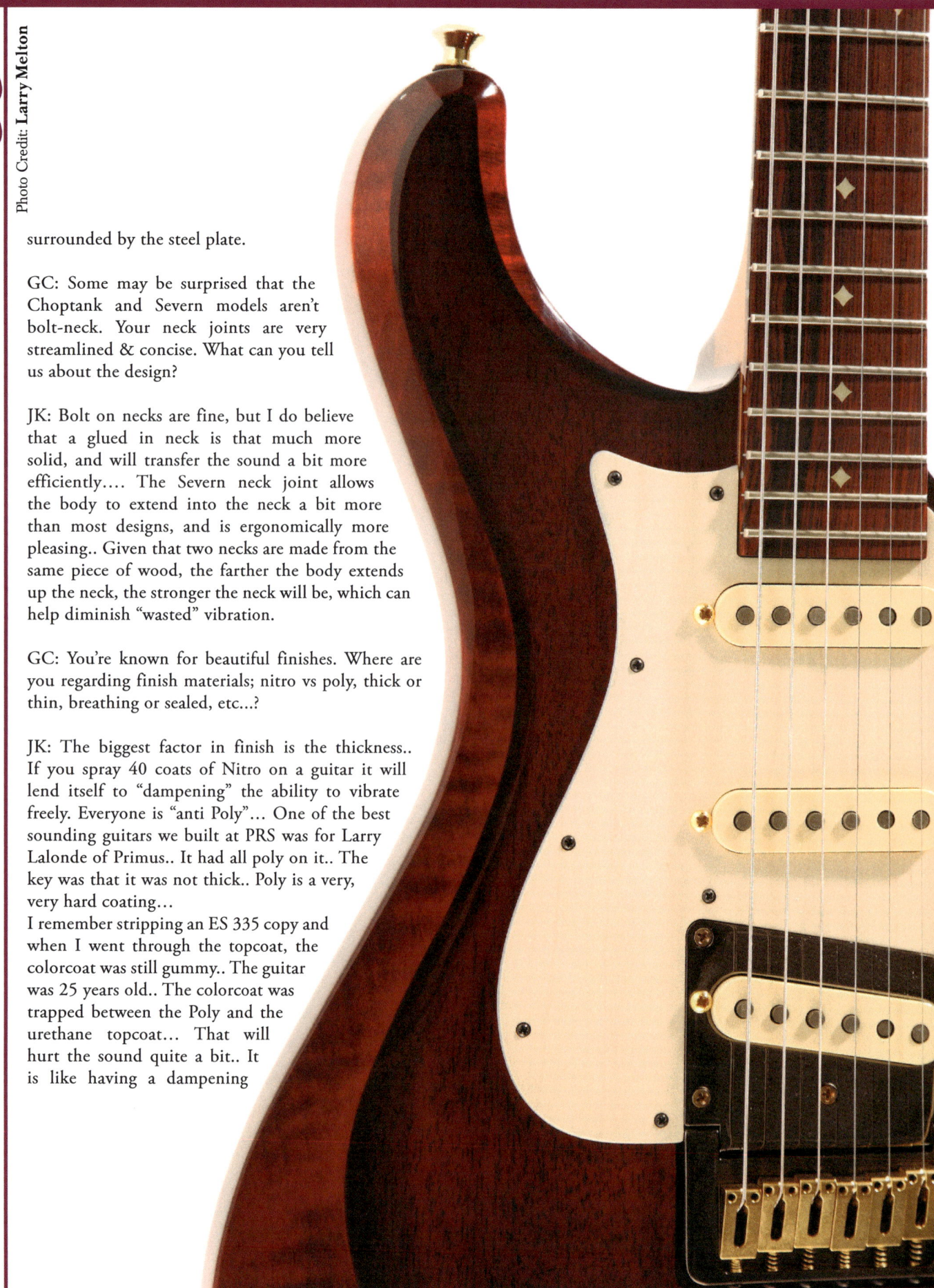

Photo Credit: **Larry Melton**

# Joe Knaggs

surrounded by the steel plate.

GC: Some may be surprised that the Choptank and Severn models aren't bolt-neck. Your neck joints are very streamlined & concise. What can you tell us about the design?

JK: Bolt on necks are fine, but I do believe that a glued in neck is that much more solid, and will transfer the sound a bit more efficiently.... The Severn neck joint allows the body to extend into the neck a bit more than most designs, and is ergonomically more pleasing.. Given that two necks are made from the same piece of wood, the farther the body extends up the neck, the stronger the neck will be, which can help diminish "wasted" vibration.

GC: You're known for beautiful finishes. Where are you regarding finish materials; nitro vs poly, thick or thin, breathing or sealed, etc...?

JK: The biggest factor in finish is the thickness.. If you spray 40 coats of Nitro on a guitar it will lend itself to "dampening" the ability to vibrate freely. Everyone is "anti Poly"… One of the best sounding guitars we built at PRS was for Larry Lalonde of Primus.. It had all poly on it.. The key was that it was not thick.. Poly is a very, very hard coating…
I remember stripping an ES 335 copy and when I went through the topcoat, the colorcoat was still gummy.. The guitar was 25 years old.. The colorcoat was trapped between the Poly and the urethane topcoat… That will hurt the sound quite a bit.. It is like having a dampening

Photo Credit: **Larry Haggard**

**Chena T1 Winter Sosltice**

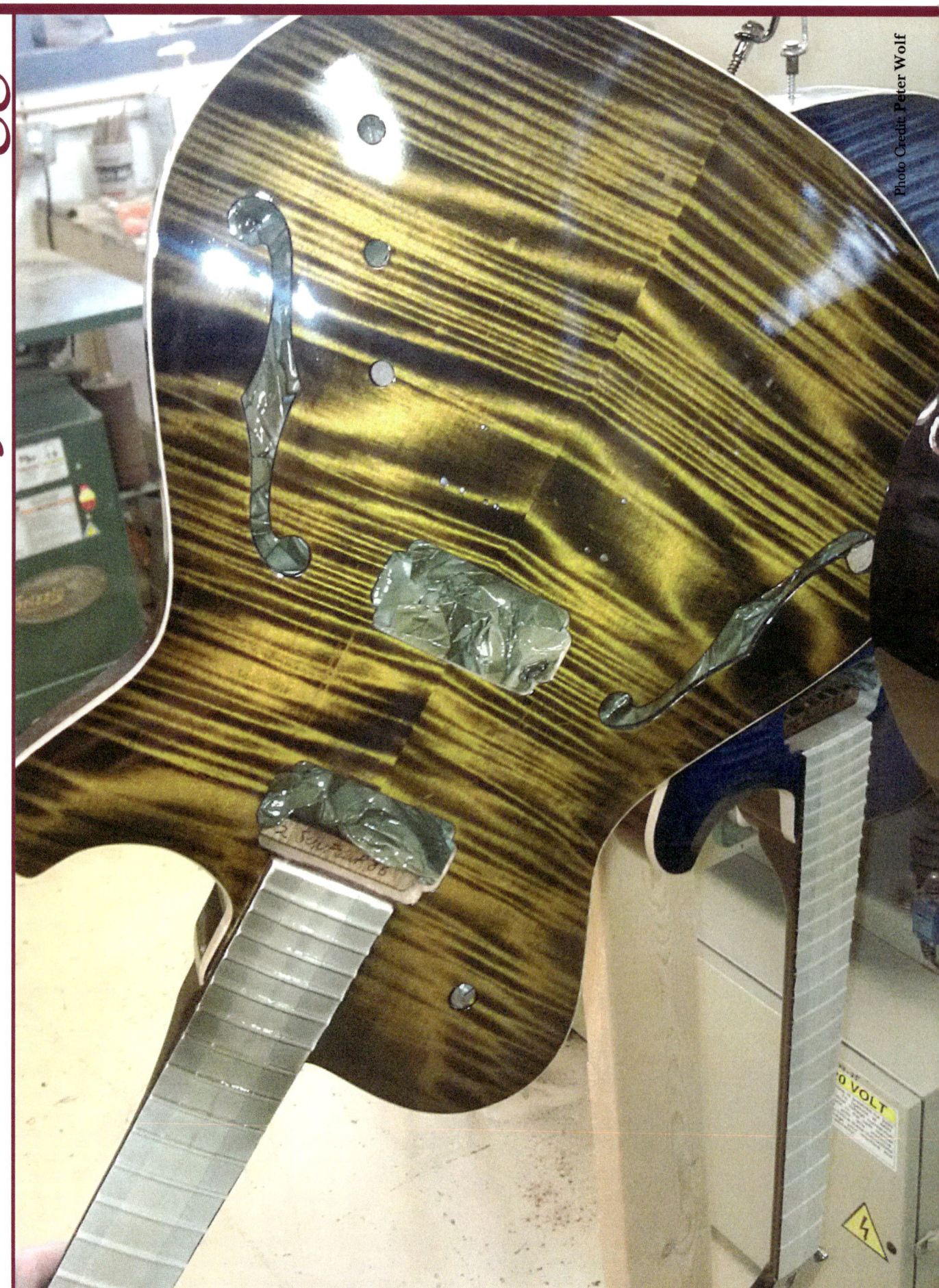

Photo Credit: Peter Wolf

# Joe Knaggs

*Knaggs Proprietary Bridge on a Kenai*

rubber between the coats…

My stand is – Keep the finish as thin as "realistically" possible, and use a coating that is not "rubber like" … It does not even have to be "rock hard"… Just cured out properly.

GC: When making multi-layered bodies, including wood pickguards, are you shooting for tonal characteristics first, followed by ways to make them look cool as well?

JK: Yes… stability is a key also.

GC: I see lots of Fralin pickups, and Duncans, right?. Do you source from anyone else-- or is there any pickup winding in-house?

JK: We do not wind our own right now… I feel that Lindy Fralin, Seymour Duncan and other pickup makers have been honing the art for quite some time, and are experts in their field. We will most likely be using "Bare Knuckle" pickups for the Steve Stevens model…

GC: With all your years of designing electric guitars, has the process of matching the right pickups for a guitar model gotten simpler for you-- or is it a long process of testing lots of pickups and crunching ideas long distance with pickup makers?

JK: I like certain sounding pickups, much like the way I feel about a guitar producing a certain sound.

It is not difficult for me to find the type of pickups we would prefer in a guitar model. Peter, John Ingram, Danny Dedo, and I have all had years and years of experience in what we think is best…

The makers I mentioned earlier have many, many different pickups to choose from, but we can also get custom pickups made from them… When I talk to Lindy, he and I usually prefer the same output levels, which I find interesting…We prefer clean, full pickups over heavily distorted ones.

Again, I do not like the pickups to have a high midrange… Steve Stevens will have the pickups he prefers in his model obviously !

GC: Bass players tend to be more open to boutique instruments. How are the basses being received so far? Are 4 strings enough for those guys?

JK: To be honest , we have not built many basses, so we have not had enough of a test field… When we do, I have some nice ideas for our basses as I learned by making mistakes with bass designs early on…

Photo Credit: Larry Melton

# Joe Knaggs

your perspectives on guitar making? While at PRS, did you work quite a bit with David Grissom?

JK: I worked with David quite a bit. He is a great guy…. It is always the key to work with guys or gals that are out there playing all the time… I had many different views given to me from the different musicians I dealt with from John Mclaughlin, John Fogerty, Tim Mahoney, to Mark Tremonti and Carlos Santana..The one thing I always found common was they would keep and continue to play an electric guitar that sounded good acoustically, so that is what you need to do first. The rest is fine tuning to their personal wants.

I am really enjoying the type of players that are choosing to play our stuff. Nils Lofgren, Stuart Fraser and Steve Stevens are the type of great players we want to be around and associated with, as well as the local and smaller venue players like Mick Hayes and Angie Swan ! We have a great group so far.

GC: Most boutique builders either do electrics or acoustics, seldom both. Clearly, your experience allows you to confront a full instrument line. Are you as comfortable with the acoustics? Does it help by providing more variety to your routine?

JK: I am very comfortable building acoustics ! I designed a nice instrument that is slightly smaller than a Dreadnaught,

Photo Credit: Guitarist Magazine, UK

and larger than an OM ... They have a great sound and are very comfortable to play. We have had many compliments on the "eveness" of the volume... It lends great variety to the routine.

GC: Besides the Tier models, is there a custom shop side?

JK: Yes, I described that earlier . My goal in the beginning phase is to build one off pieces that I create on my own... We will consider the "Custom shop " side after that.

GC: We're starting to see more things like thermal treated woods, compensated nuts & frets, stainless steel frets and the PLEK machine. Any thoughts on some of these approaches?

JK: Billions of albums were sold off songs that were played on the guitars that we know and grew up with – no compensated nuts, no stainless steel fretwire, no Plek! The guitars that are going for 200K like pre war Martins, 59 Les Pauls had none of these things. I do think that all these things are good innovations, and each one has it's own thing which much is personal preference... For instance – I hate stainless steel fretwire. I would never even consider fretting my own guitar with it, but that is my own take. I remember recording with a friend of mine Todd Kreuzburg who is an amazing guitar player. We tuned the guitar that had a compensated nut with a strobe tuner. I played and we both agreed that the d note on the b string did not sound right as well as a few other notes, so we retuned the guitar using our ears and everything was fine...It is so much in your touch, what your ears are used to and preference.

GC: You joined PRS during their first year with about as many staff as you have onboard now. Considering your experience and improvements in technology, you have many reasons to be optimistic. Do you plan to stay in R&D and building as much as possible while bringing in good admin staff to wear most of the business hats?

JK: Yes, that is the way I would like to have it, my skills are in designing and creating. Peter's skills are in marketing, sales, etc.

# Joe Knaggs

Photo Credit: **Peter Wolf**

**Joe showing off a finished acoustic**

*Black Natural Choptank T2*

Danny's skills are in programming, jig making etc., If we are number crunching, purchasing, office working, etc., we are not taking advantage of the skills god gave us, which is not best for the company.

GC: We're also interviewing your marketing partner Peter Wolf. Do you brainstorm quite a bit with Peter?

JK: All the time! I brainstorm with everyone here as well... That is how you get the best results.

GC: We see you building an artist roster, most notably Steve Stevens... Has it helped gain any significant attention this early on?

JK: The only thing more important than having artists play your stuff is creating a great product. Nike did not even make golf equipment until Tiger Woods came along.. Now it is huge! Of course if they made crap, it would not have much staying power, and realistically would make Tiger look like a farce.

GC: On a day when everything is going right at Knaggs Guitars, in which areas/tasks are you having the most fun?

JK: Good way of starting the question ! I really enjoy working on acoustics, but the best part is dealing with the guys that I work with. We laugh a lot while getting a great level of work done.. There

is not much better in life than getting projects accomplished with a great group of people.

GC: How many more rivers do you hope to cross (or fish) by 2020?

JK: Hard one to answer... Lots

GC: Anything else you want our readers to know about what's in store from Knaggs Guitars?

JK: The main thing I always want to convey is how proud and appreciative I/we are of what WE have accomplished, and that my wife Leslie and family have been wonderful through all of it...It has been a bear, and EVERYONE involved has made an impact... Now the business is somewhat out of the "start up" phase I/we will be getting into the design mode again, which will bring new products and processes.

My mind is always churning with new artwork, material ideas etc., and we will be moving forward with all of it.

www.knaggsguitars.com

# Knaggs Kenai Review

## Gc Test Drives the Knaggs Kenai

JP Holesworth

We had a special opportunity to play with a dazzling new Kenai for a bit. Did I just say "dazzling"? Why yes, I did. Maybe it was the nitro fumes when opening the case that pulled me into the curly maple, trans forest green tint top. Combine that with a mahogany platform of regal weight, this LP-type was strong and balanced whether unplugged or striding through a tube circuit into a 2-12 combo.

Pickups are Duncan HB's... SH-2's I think. Don't worry about it ok, they're some kind of vintage voice variant of a PAF. Who can keep track anyway. Most important is that the guitar looks great and sounds great! And I really hate throwing "great" around like that, especially after already using dazzling.

Through a Marshall JCM 600 combo I never kicked in my very fav-o-rite OD pedal. A little taste thru a '66 Vibrolux... But a higher volume locale opportunity lie with the 600 where I was able to push Grissom-like tones with just some delay along for fun. Don't dare forget that Joe Knaggs knows something about Grissom-like tones. But let's unplug for a minute and behold more than a surplus amount of vibration from head to butt (feels better than "toe"). And I dig toes too, but this Tier 2 Kenai is all about legs... tennis girl legs at that!

When a hefty-side mahogany unit in this craft range is alive with resonance, you start to anticipate an exciting plugged in experience. Feels like an automobile review, huh. Well ok then, handling is nimble and tight in the curves with adequate stiffness from a highly tuned suspension. Neck is big but shaped for moving around. Body is thinner than an LP, or at least it's

contoured in back for overall slimmer attitude.

Headstock angle is way less than expected, but made up for at the bridge end where a sharp breaking angle- from saddles to tailpiece section- joins the bridge and allows for ample string pressure to build more resonance. Perhaps the mild headstock angle rescues some added string bending travel in order to offset breakage issues at the saddles. Just my guess—though I could be totally off here. The standard tune-o-matic bridge merges into a unique yet unassuming tailpiece design that many traditionalists shouldn't flag. I did more of a triple take myself, it's so clean and natural.

Did we digress at "Grissom-like tones…"?

A chunky '59 style neck with 12" radius and medium frets declares every note
with authority. I'm serious too. And this guitar hits the amp with a big, sweet balance that sings and compresses while maintaining strong definition. Bridge and middle positions are particularly articulate & soulful with big balls for Blues and Rock territories. Neck is typical, so grab the Wah pedal. The Kenai sounds and feels as bold as it looks; combining classic lines with tasteful modern contours and fresh Knaggs cues. But the real key is a build process that gets every step right, resulting in a guitar integrated for superlative voicing and playability. Yeah, I really liked it!

The "Tier 2" model tested was nicely appointed with gold finish hardware, scrape maple body binding, open back tuners and an artsy little inlay shape they call "morning star" for the position markers & headstock. Listing at $5.5k, the Knaggs Kenai T2 brings big personality, top shelf fit & finish and flawless set-up with just a touch of bling… Tennis girl legs and Grissom-like tones!

Peter Wolf

Photo Credit: Helmut Scheven

Branding Guru

Entrepeneur

Guitarist

Peter Wolf is one of the music industry's hardest working people. He played a key role in introducing PRS Guitars (Paul Reed Smith), on a global scale to guitarists, and has done everything from distribution, to artist relations to brand building. And he continues to do so consistently after 25 years. In 2010 he joined forces with master luthier Joe Knaggs to launch their own company simply called "Knaggs Guitars".

Photo Credit: Left to right: **Michael G. Stewart, Michael G. Stewart, Peter Staaden**

# Peter Wolf

Photo Credit: Aldo Garcia Solares

*Never to busy for a little family time. (Left to Right) Peter Wolf and son Lucas Wolf*

Joe Knaggs has created a line of exquisite instruments, which are all built by hand, and to a very high standard... That's right, no offshore budget lines here! And Peter Wolf is standing with him to help ensure that Joe's vision does not get sidetracked, and emphasis on craftsmanship is always the priority.

In just 2 short years, Knaggs has secured their spot as a top contender in guitar innovation, global sales, and artist acceptance. As always, Joe Knaggs and Peter Wolf are about obtaining big results.

GC: With a business and marketing background, how did you end up in the music industry?

PW: I got into music and playing instruments early on as a kid, although I never had lessons. Growing up in a musical household certainly helped. My Dad was a self taught piano and violin player, and my sister and brothers all played instruments. There was always music in our house although soccer was probably more of a passion of mine growing up. After high school, I did an apprenticeship at a local insurance and banking company while attending business school. I got drafted into the German army when I was done with my education, while friends of mine had started Prosound Music

Center in Koblenz, Germany, which was a 1500 square foot store in the beginning. We had made plans for me to join the company once I was out of service, and I started as a partner in 1978. I had been playing drums and guitars in bands for a while, but becoming a partner in a music store made me take musical instruments more seriously. I started practicing and paying attention to what other people were doing. Since I was the guitar sales guy, I had to learn everything about the gear I was selling, which also included being able to play at a reasonable level.

GC: Why was PRS the right company to work with at the time?

PW: By 1980 we had moved to a fully fledged 10,000 square feet facility, and things were going really well. We would find and import US products and put them on the map in Europe. It was the time of wild colors, graphics and pointed headstocks (laughs)! I had already successfully been importing and marketing Hamer guitars and other US brands in Central Europe for almost a decade when one of our customers made me aware of PRS. So I flew to Chicago to attend the Summer NAMM Show 1986, introduced myself to Paul and got the line as one of three exclusive dealers in Germany. About a year later, I was doing most of the business

Peter Wolf

Photo Credit: Markus Kaes

and was granted exclusive distributorship for Germany, Austria and Luxembourg. Another three years later, I founded PRS Guitars Germany, and solely focused on distribution, brand building and marketing of PRS, Soldano, Lakland and other high-end US products. Our relationship and friendship got deeper, and eventually led to my direct engagement with PRS, USA in 1997, first as their International Sales Manager and later as their Director of Global Sales & Marketing.

GC: Having gained a significant amount of experience in both the European and American markets; what are some of the differences you've noticed between consumers of high-end musical instruments in the two markets?

PW: I don't think there are main differences as far as consumers are concerned. People who appreciate quality and well made instruments live everywhere. The individual market size, though and the number of people who can afford high quality, more expensive instruments, are mainly a question of disposable income, which has traditionally been higher in the US, Europe and Japan.

GC: Working side by side with Joe for so many years what were your PRS days like?

PW: Between 1997 and 2003 (Peter moved to the US in July 2003), I was going back and forth. I would be in town for several weeks or months at a time and then go back to Europe or travel to other parts of the World to find potential distributors and dealers, and create substantial relationships.

Joe and I were part of PRS' senior executive team and worked together closely on different projects, and eventually we became friends and hung out whenever I was in town. We would attend trade shows together and travel the World to promote sales. We also started clinics and seminars, in which Joe would carve guitars and talk about every aspect of

designing and building instruments. I learned a lot about guitar making from him, and he probably learned a few things from me as well. We have a similar approach when it comes to working with people.

GC: Since the launch of Knaggs in 2010, we've seen Knaggs grow exponentially from the expansion of the product line, artists, and dealers. It takes some luthiers 10 plus years to get to where you have taken Knaggs in only 2 short years. Can you elaborate on the secret sauce here without giving away your recipe?

PW: It always starts with a vision. Joe's vision was to design and create his own line of instruments and focus on his preferences and ideas. As a designer and builder- as an artist- at some point you want to sign your own paintings. I have worked with most high-end guitar makers of our time in the past decades. Joe is certainly one of the best. He's totally hands on, can do it all and is involved in every aspect of creating and building great instruments. He is also humble, moderate and easy going, which always helps.

My vision was and is to making Knaggs Guitars a respected, honorable and profitable company, to getting our creations out there in working with artists, dealers and distributors, and to build strong relationships with everyone who's part of the journey. I like communicating with people on all levels in our industry. The rest is hard work and persistence.

GC: Speaking of hard work and persistence, What were some of the challenges you and Joe faced when launching Knaggs from the ground up, and how did you overcome them?

PW: We started Knaggs Guitars at the end of 2009, in the midst of a really bad economical climate. I'm not going to talk much about financial institutions, banks and what caused the mayhem. We all know, more or less what happened and how it happened.

Peter Wolf

*Knaggs Fam left to right: With Stuart Fraser's guitar right after completion: Lukas Fronzoli, John Ingram, Danny Dedo, Peter Wolf, Joe Knaggs, Scott Shirley, Will Schuyler.*

*Missing is Dean Nitsch and Steven Baumgardner who took the shot.*

*(Pictured Left to right) Joe & Peter Receiving the MS Award for Best new Manufacturer 2011*

However, it really affected start-ups and smaller companies. You couldn't get a loan to save your life. But... we knew good people who were willing to help; who liked and believed in what we had to offer and who wanted to be part of it.

They still are part of the tribe and have become good friends and associates in the mean time. Besides financials, literally everything had to be done. We had to find a building, get machines, tools and equipment, purchase wood, materials, build benches, create work space, tables, racks, and everything else you need when you are trying to make guitars.

It was a huge undertaking, and Joe and Danny and later Dean and the rest of the team did a phenomenal job in getting it going.

I was mainly focusing on getting the word out, building networks, engaging individuals, distributors, dealers, players and media and making everyone aware who we are and what we are doing.

GC: Do you have a hand in the design process of Knaggs-- or is it all up to Joe?

PW: A little bit. I'm not good at drawing, you know. I find it very difficult to draw what I call 'classic shapes'. I could probably draw some outside stuff (laughs) but when it comes to shapes that have potential to become classic shapes, you need someone who knows what they are doing.

I always provide input and my take, though for what it's worth. I have a certain view and perception when it comes to lines or proportions. I may not be very good in coming up with designs but I'm usually doing okay in evaluating their potential.

GC: I'm going to play devil's advocate here as to how Knaggs may be perceived...ready? How different are Knaggs from PRS guitars? I mean c'mon really, it's the private stock guy with a few new shapes and a different name...no?

*Peter Wolf keeps the branding going with Knaggs guitar pics*

PW: I'm sure there are people out there who think or say that. It is fairly known that Joe designed a number of models at PRS and has been instrumental in getting them into production. As Director of R&D and Private Stock he certainly had his hands in pretty much everything that came out of there in the past 2 decades.

Our line is very different, though. First of all, we are using classic scale lengths (25.5 inch for Chesapeake, 24.75 inch for Influence line instruments). All of our guitars have set necks. We offer both 3-on a-side as well as 6-on-a-side headstocks. The Influence line consisting of single and double cutaway guitars with humbuckers including hollowbodies, features carved mahogany backs and carved maple tops.

We also offer single coil equipped guitars with the Chesapeake line, single and double cut, with flat or beveled tops and wooden pickguards. Last but not least, we have been building some amazing acoustics and basses as well.

To me, there is a good variety of body and head stock shapes and models, appointments and different tones within our line. I feel our bridge designs are unique and special and have a lot to do with

how our guitars sound. Plus there are few conceptual innovations and ideas that make a difference.

GC: So let's talk about proof of concept to a full line model roll out. What kind of research went into the Knaggs line? Why did these shapes work? And finally how different were the prototypes to what we see today?

PW: Well, keep in mind we have been around high-end guitars for a long time. I guess what I'm trying to say is there is a level of experience and knowledge that comes with the years. We had many conversations over a period of 2-3 months and really dug into the history of guitars and what we were into.

The Choptank, Severn and Acoustic Patuxent already existed when we started drawing the other models. When I say we, I mean Joe drawing and me watching him lol! We both felt it was important to add a line of carved maple top instruments, which led to the Influence line Kenai, Keya, Chena and Sheyenne models. Joe just drew them. I know it sounds funny but he did. He drew them and we kept looking at the drawings in his workshop for weeks, and made minor changes here and there until we felt we got it right.

# Peter Wolf

# Peter Wolf

Photo Credit: **Andy Fuchs**

*(Pictured Left to right) Joe & Peter at one of the many trade shows they attend every year*

It took several months to get all designs and drawings completed, and then Joe and Danny built each one by hand. I remember thinking a few times while we were at it that I'm watching birth. The initial prototypes we made and introduced in March 2010 in Frankfurt, Germany were all part of our current line. I think we used a medium rubbed out (nitro) finish for the 9 instruments we took to Germany, though.

GC: I read an interview with you where you clearly stated "We are not reinventing the wheel here" yet, looking through the shapes, the designs are different enough for any avid player to feel at home with them, yet they possess a fresh approach to something new. Were the guitars designed to be functional and that is what determined the shape, or where the shapes done first and then you guys went to work making them functional?

PW: Well, most shapes that have caught on were designed back in the 17th and 18th century in Italy. There aren't many shapes left to be drawn that can make it into the hall of fame in my humble opinion. I think Joe is somebody who can. When it comes to guitars, I think it is looks and sound, in that order. If I'm not attracted to a specific shape, or dislike certain lines, I won't pick it up. Once I do pick it up, I get the feel for the neck, fret work, ergonomics, balance and weight, and then at some point how it sounds acoustically and amplified.

For me, it always starts with the shape. Making it functional and great sounding is part of the process, although it is a huge task, too. On that end, Joe and the team have a very good track record.

GC: Walk us through the quality assurance at the Knaggs factory...

PW: We have good people with a lot of experience in making great guitars. Everyone knows what they are doing. Plus, Joe is there every day and works closely with everyone.

GC: Any plans for an overseas line?

PW: No.

cfjphoto.com

*Artist Steve Stevens with a Kenai Tier 2*

GC: You will be launching a Steve Stevens signature Kenai model at Musikmesse Germany next month. Tell us about this guitar and how this collaboration came about?

PW: I had known Steve since the early 80s when he had his signature models with Hamer. I always thought he was one of the best players out there, and somebody who really appreciates and understands guitars. After we had started the company, we first had to find a shop and get all the needed equipment, which took a while.

I think I contacted Steve late 2011 and we started talking. Joe had made him a few PRS before so Steve was very familiar with Joe and his work. We first sent him a double cut Keya, which he liked but Steve preferred a single cut with a thicker body and a slightly narrower neck since he has been playing Les Paul's in recent years.

So we built him a guitar based on our Kenai model, incorporating his preferences and specs. And he used the guitar on Billy Idol's 2012 European tour.

That led to us talking about a signature model.

GC: Why is Steve Stevens the "right" candidate to endorse a signature Kenai?

PW: Besides being one of the most talented and respected players, a Grammy-Award winning Artist, writer, composer and major collaborator, Steve is a total gear head. He really cares about his instruments, amps, his equipment and his sound, and he knows all about it. For us, it is a big deal to work with someone of his caliber and to be put to his test.

GC: Where do you see Knaggs in the next 10 years?

PW: I don't think that far lol ... I'm taking it day by day. I hope we are still around making instruments, playing music and hanging out with our friends and associates. Everything else is a bonus.

GC: Thanks so much for taking the time to talk to us Peter.

www.brandwolf.net

# Steve Stevens on Knaggs & Beyond –

by: Kelcey Alonzo & Antoine Gedroyc

Steve Stevens

Photo Credit: **Larry Melton**

We all know the stories, the glam rock stage pictures and the blazing cinematic riffs that left a mark on Rock n' Roll history.

Preparing this issue's feature on Knaggs Guitars came with a bonus opportunity to speak with the legendary Steve Stevens. Currently working with Knaggs on a signature model guitar, Steve was gracious enough to share about this project and his gear. But first, we also take a quick journey through a fascinating life and career including a love of flamenco and classical guitar playing, which many might not associate him with. Solo albums like Flamenco.A.Go.Go and Memory Crash display a diverse virtuosity with all the Rebel Yell/Danger Zone fire Stevens is famous for.

A short 15-20 min interview turned into 45 minutes of conversation, and a most enjoyable time for all. Steve is truly an amazing person; accessible, humble and passionate about music, instruments and people.

# Steve Stevens

Photo Credit: **Charles Jischke**

*Steve Stevens live*

Guitar Connoisseur: What first piqued your interest in music? Never mind the guitar for now, let's stick to your musical interests.

Steve Stevens: My parents were very much into music, although they didn't play any instrument. The very 1st concert they took me to was Dave Brubeck. We always shared music in my household. My dad has a very extensive record collection. He would bring the 1st albums with Moog synthesizers home, and was really into electronics and electronic music way before it was considered to be "cool". Our house was always buzzing with some kind of music.

GC: So when did the guitar bug bite you?

SS: Well as a kid I never really envisioned myself making a living out of this. Growing up in Far Rockaway, NY, just outside of NYC, there was a famous protest musician called Phil Ochs. Everyone in my neighborhood was really enamored with Phil. His sister was actually my first guitar teacher.

The mid 60's were the years of the singer/songwriter, and everyone around me was playing guitar. I started playing when I was just about seven and a half years old, but it wasn't until I was 13 that I picked up an electric guitar. I would be playing folk music on a very cheap $13 beginner's guitar.

It was a really horrible guitar that came with a little booklet, but it did the job. Within 6 months of that my parents got me a better instrument, a nylon string again for about $100. Playing guitar was just the cool thing to do.

We grew up about a half a mile from the beach. My older brother played, all my friends played, so in the summer everyone would be on the beach playing guitar, and I guess I just wanted to be a part of it.

Playing bass and keyboards only came much later down the road, out of a necessity. You wouldn't believe how many of your favorite albums involve the guitar player recording the bass part. There is something really special about that though. Having the same person with the same DNA playing both the guitar and bass parts make them fuse together into almost an instrument of its own. Somebody had to do it! (laughs)

GC: Take us through the "Steve Stevens" pedagogy of learning how to play. What methods of learning and practicing got you where you are today?

SS: My first real teacher, when I was about 10 years old at summer camp, was a flamenco player. I didn't know what this particular style was called but it touched me, and the energy level, the emotion and expressivity blew me away. Still, to this day I love nylon string guitars.

*Knaggs Steve Stevens Signature Headstocks*

GC: Do you see strong similarities between metal and other modern genres and the flamenco?

SS: Absolutely! I've often described flamenco as the speed metal of classical guitar myself! I started playing folk music on nylon string guitars, then studied classical and flamenco very early. It is like a natural loop to go back to the roots and record Flamenco. A. Go. Go.

GC: So what led you to pick up the electric guitar?

SS: Probably just hearing things on the radio. And I had an uncle whose job was to service juke boxes. He would bring a stack of about a hundred different 45's; The Stones, Hendrix, Motown, all these kind of things. I thought, "Wow! if I want to sound like that, I m going to need an electric guitar!" When I was about 13 my parents got me a Univox electric guitar, a Univox amp and an Electro-Harmonix "Big Muff" as one package.

GC: So once you got the gear how did you learn to play the electric?

SS: Hmm, I would say for electric I was pretty much self-taught. I continued to have a classical guitar teacher. I went to the High School of Performing Arts of NY (The school the movie "Fame" was based on), and in order to get in, I had to play a classical piece. As far as the electric guitar goes, it was really hard to find any kind of teacher back then. You had to find older kids who would play in the neighborhood you know... Most of the time you had to listen to the records over and over; slowing them down to try and understand what they were doing!

Steve Stevens

SS: I don't necessarily think that it's how you learn, but more what you learn... the material that you learn. The stuff that I was spending countless hours learning, trying to figure it out, was not what most people were trying to duplicate.

For some reason I was always interested in things that were "out of the box". By the time I was 13, there was a radio station in NY called WNEW. They had a show called "Things from England", and they'd play the latest Genesis, Emerson Lake and Palmer and Yes. I really fell in love with that new genre of Progressive Rock. Those guitarists were - to me - playing all of the styles that I was learning; classical, blues, rock, jazz in a very non-academic way. I think it was just a matter of having my mind open and wanting to play other styles. Keith Emerson would talk about classical music. I remember I didn't know who John Coltrane was until I read an interview of Allan Holdsworth talking about him, so I thought "Oh! Who's that? I want to learn THAT!"

To this day I always tell players and musicians how important it always has been to me to learn, love and appreciate styles and genres outside of what you are going to play. People still ask me to this day things like, "How did you come up with the intro to Rebel Yell?" Well, that was me emulating Keith Emerson you know... I could say it's my love of things outside of guitar that led me to come up with these parts. I wasn't trying to be anyone else but myself, even though I loved listening to all these guys; Hendrix, Page, Emerson and so many others, but I wasn't trying to be any of them.

GC: How did you and Billy Idol team up?

SS: Billy had come from an English punk rock kind of background. I think the last thing he needed was another punk rock guitar player. He'd already done 3 records with Generation X. He and his producer Keith Wilson were really looking for someone to bring something different. We just hung out as mates really at first, talking about music we loved and getting to know each other. I remember talking about Lou Reed and Bowie.

This whole dynamic between the singer and the guitar player was very important. He understood that deeply. We pretty much then got right down to writing songs. He had a record to do, and I said, "Well, let's do this!"

GC: That leads us towards the creative dynamics between the two of you. How did/do you work together?

SS: Even to this day, it's always different. There is no set rule or protocol for me to go about writing songs. "Rebel Yell", for example, was just Billy and I sitting in the studio, thinking, "Ok, we have to come up with a great rock'n roll song." But "Eyes Without a Face" was completely different. I came up with the music, living in my parent's basement at the time. The only radio station I could get was an "oldie station". They'd play things like Frankie Valli, and I thought it would be nice to do something with those kinds of chords changes. I brought that to the rehearsal, and Billy had the lyrics that were just a perfect fit.

Photo Credit: **Chrles Jischke**

cfjphoto.com

*Tier 2 Kenai Steve Stevens tested on the road*

Obviously my job as a guitar player is to help the singer tell a story. I'm not here to make myself shine-- but serve the song. And if I'm doing my job well, we'd end up with a good one !

GC: Does having a lot of different amps, effects and guitars help in this creative process? Find the right pen to write the right story?

SS: You can write a song on any guitar really. It's nice to have different guitars and gear that I've accumulated over the years. I just love guitars! There is nothing cooler to me than opening the case of a new guitar! It's just doing it for me... they are great for me.

I had 3 cars in my entire life, they just don't do it for me (laughs). But guitars always did and still do to this day! I just love everything about them. I remember my first Les Paul was a tobacco sunburst Standard '73 or '74, and as soon as I grabbed it I felt that this was a "real" guitar you know. It fit my hand right, the neck felt right, the body style was small. It felt just right, and better than pretty much anything I had before.

GC: Most recently you partnered up with Knaggs Guitars and started touring with a Kenai model. How did this collaboration come about?

SS: I had known Peter (Peter Wolf of Knaggs Guitars) for probably 29 years. He was involved with Hamer Guitars way back in the day.

My best memories with Hamer Guitars, was going to Germany, to the Frankfurt Musikmesse (music gear trade show). He had arranged for me to play with John Entwistle and Zak Starkey.

We sort of stayed in contact since, and it was only natural that he approached me when he got involved with Knaggs. I didn't really know Joe but I owned a couple PRS Guitars.

When Peter emailed me and told me Joe was one of the custom shop guys at PRS, and mentioned some of the features of Knaggs such as the "one piece bridge", I knew exactly what he was talking about.

GC: So that quickly led to developing your own Signature model?

SS: Well I said, "Look if you'd like to go down this road with me, there are a couple of things I'd like changed, but I'd love to work with you."

The best thing about Knaggs is that they never said no to anything I could come up with. They never made excuses for anything. I wanted to have a very special custom binding on the guitar, in the spirit of a pearloid drum kit. They said sure, even though they never worked with this material before. I gave them the neck shape, profile, nut width of my favorite Les Paul, and they nailed it on the first time. I wanted a thicker body than the original Knaggs they had sent me and a few more

Photo Credit: **Peter Wolf**

*Steve Stevens Special Bindings*

changes. I really felt they were putting a lot of passion and energy into this, and were as excited as I was about it.

GC: Was the thicker body an ergonomic or a sound concern... or a little bit of both?

SS: Absolutely, a little bit of both. I really like a "substantial" guitar. I just can't get used to the whole chambering thing. I am not saying they are good or bad, it's just not my thing. I don't think they sound the same. That's one of the things I discussed with Joe. The selection of the "right" mahogany, and keeping the guitar right around 8 lbs was critical.

GC: The weight of the guitar for you is a very important factor?

SS: Very much so. I don't feel comfortable with super light, featherweight light instruments. I didn't want the guitar to be too heavy either. To me right around 8 lbs is an ideal balanced weight; not too light, not too heavy. I said, "Look I also like really heavy jumbo frets on my guitars. I'm not going to lie, and try and make a guitar that everybody likes." I really wanted it to stay true to my personal specs and preferences... keep its strong personality and character. That's what I play and if people dig it, then great!

GC: So you were deeply involved in the design and specs!

SS: Exactly, it wasn't about licensing my name or just having a decal on the back of the headstock that says "Steve Stevens Signature" (laughs)! It was made very clear from day one that the guitar should be a very high quality instrument; no cheaper Korean or Chinese fabrication, but everything is coming out of Knaggs' shop. I really never wanted to compromise with the quality and specs. And again, they never said no to anything I was requesting. It's going to be made

Steve Stevens

Photo Credit: Charles Jischke

in very limited numbers initially, and if there is a demand for it great! It is a superb, super high quality guitar, it's the tool that I use, and if other people dig it too, all the better!

GC: What other main changes can we disclose vs the stock Kenai?

SS: The pickups are Bare Knuckle hand wound. I chose not to use my "Rebel Yell" (also by BK) that I love as a Les Paul replacement pickup. But I had to be honest, and didn't like them as much with this particular build. Even though it's a great pickup, it didn't sound right to me in this guitar; it became a little bit too honky.

The Knaggs responds differently than a traditional Les Paul, it does have more bottoms and tops, and the bridge delivers an amazing dynamic, a lot of sustain. I wanted to go with lower wound, AlNiCo magnets pickups, something a tad less brutal/aggressive, to balance the personality and voice of the instrument. We went through 4 or 5 different pick up versions, and just this week I decided the ones I felt were a perfect match.

GC: How do you A/B test so many pickups?

SS: To me, the tell/tell is the middle position, using the both pickups together. When it comes together right, it's almost like a gigantic acoustic guitar. Lots of instruments just don't sound right on this position. Beautiful expressivity, balance-- you can play all these kinds of chords, arpeggios, single notes, and you always get an amazing clarity and tone.

**GC: If we could sum it up, what would you say about this Steve Stevens Signature model?**

SS: It really came together out of a genuine friendship. It didn't come out as a business adventure. It really is the combination of an artist and a company who want to put a very high quality guitar out there. Mutual respect, friendship... a lot of successful things originate out of friendship you know! I love picking up and playing this guitar, it puts a huge smile on my face.

GC: What do you have coming up in 2013?

SS: We are working with Billy, writing new material for a new record right now. He has an auto-biography coming out so we're hoping to have the record ready at the same time. Actually as soon as we're done here, we're going to work together today.

GC: Thank you very much for talking to us!

SS: Thanks for supporting guitars! To me it's still the greatest instrument in the world; it still has magic, man!

http://stevestevens.bigcartel.com/

Steve Stevens

# Steve Stevens Signature Knaggs – Gallery

Photo Credit: **Larry Melton**

Steve Stevens

Steve Stevens

Steve Stevens

Photo Credit: Larry Melton

# Photographers Vault

**Derek Brad** is an acclaimed photographer from the metropolitan Philadelphia area. His childhood passion for drawing, sketching and illustrating led to a lifelong urge to create and capture images. Derek's music photography is recognized around the world for its ability to bring the viewer into the electricity and excitement of a concert experience. This led to his current positions as the house photographer at the Mann Center for the Performing Arts and the Trocadero Theater and he is a regular contributor to Revolver, Rolling Stone, and Rhyme Street magazines, among many others.

Today, Derek has earned a reputation for doing whatever it takes tocapture the passion of a performance, the personality of an entertainer or the essence of a brand. However, Derek is more than just a music photographer. He enjoys challenging himself by taking on projects in advertising, editorial and conceptual portraiture as well as personalprojects like Musician Portrait Project and Where is Derek Brad's Aston Martin.

The future for Derek Brad is another empty frame, wall, magazine, book, gallery, website, billboard or building waiting to be filled with Derek's imaginative and innovative work.

**Subject:** Slash
**Date:** May 20, 2012
**Camera:** Canon 7D
**Location:** Susquehanna Bank Center Camden, NJ

"One of my personal favorite musicians of all time. When he came to the front to play his solo I wanted to get right up under the Gibson and get the photograph looking up at a Legend. A bonus that I like about this photograph is the way his sunglasses reflect the half indoor/half outdoor venue. It gives the glasses an extra glow."

Photographers Vault

**Subject:** Buckethead
**Date:** March 31, 2012
**Camera:** Canon 5D
**Location:** Trocadero Theatre  Philadelphia, Pa

"Wanted to capture Buckethead
with his signature Les Paul"

Photographers Vault

**Subject:** Dave Navarro (Janes Addiction)
**Date:** June 5, 2009
**Camera:** Canon 40D
**Location:** Susuquehanna Bank Center  Camden, NJ

"The lighting was great for this tour and I wanted to get a lot of great images of the entire band, which did turn out to be a wonderful set."

# Photographers Vault

**Subject:** Gary Clark Jr.
**Date:** November 10, 2012
**Camera:** Canon 5D Mark II
**Location:** Theatre of Living Arts  Philadelphia, Pa

"Wanted to capture a close up of Gary Clark Jr to get his soul and passion he creates with his guitar"

# Photographers Vault

**Subject:** Tommy Thayer of KISS
**Date:** October 12, 2009
**Camera:** Canon 5D
**Location:** Wachovia Center Philadelphia, Pa

"Wanted to get a great portrait of Thayer's face because a lot of KISS fans that I'm friends with still feel uneasy seeing him in the Ace face paint."

"Paul running down the stage. I really like the color that the crowd projected on the screen gives off in this photograph."

**Subject:** Paul Stanley of KISS
**Date:** October 12, 2009
**Camera:** Canon 5D
**Location:** Wachovia Center Philadelphia, PA

# Photographers Vault

**Subject:** Pete Loeffler of Chevelle
**Date:** August 3, 2012
**Camera:** Canon 5D Mark II
**Location:** House Of Blues  Atlantic City, NJ

"A lot of energy and action.  The band was places rather far back on the stage so when Pete came all the way to the edge I couldn't miss this opportunity. I dropped down to the ground at the same time switched from my long lens camera to my camera with the wide angle and captured him only inches away from the camera."

# Doug Rappoport

# AN HOUR WITH SCOTT HENDERSON

*"A mind that is stretched by a new experience can never go back to its old dimensions."* -Oliver Wendell Holmes, Jr.

This is not an interview with Scott Henderson. This is a just an anecdote; an account of an hour with a master.

I teach at GIT in Hollywood, usually once a week. I love the people there. The instructors are knowledgeable and willing to help, the program is solid, and most of the kids are alright too, mamma. It's a cool vibe.

The best part is that two doors down from my little teaching cove, in the big room, is Scott Henderson. Now, to me, you can't talk about the top 5 greatest fusion guitar players ever and not include Scott Henderson in that conversation. For my money (and this is personal preference), Scott is the THE best. I've thought that since I was a kid.

My first day teaching at GIT (like 5 years ago!), I ran into Scott in the hallway. I put out my hand and told him what a great honor it was to meet him. He was kind and

*Doug Rappoport, Pro Musician*

invited me to his Open Counceling (OC).

10 minutes later I walked in the staff room and he looked up at me from the lunch table and said, "Hey man you can't be in here!" I showed him I was staff, and he laughed and it was all good.

So over my years and a billion students, many come to my room, guitar in hand and say, in a billion different languages, "I want to learn Fusion". I look at them like they're crazy. Then I give them my stock answer, "... Dude! 2 doors down is the greatest *Fusion guitar player on the planet and he is having an OC session all day.

Why the *%#* are you asking ME to teach you Fusion??!" -- Yeah, Roger Clemens lives next door to me, and I'm going across the street to ask old man Perkins, the retired history teacher, how to throw a fastball.... UH-DERRRRRR! Not that I'm an old history teacher... but you get the idea.

How bitchin' is it that these kids come to this school, and cats like Scott Henderson are there show them everything? So why is his room so empty???
Scott plays with the door wide open and as loud as he wants. No one dares tell him to turn down. He's Scott Henderson. When you walk in the room, a few brave souls have their guitars out awaiting their turns to take a solo after Scott. Then they wait to hear Scott say, "That was good." OR "You shouldn't be here. You better go back and learn X, Y, Z..." Scott pulls no punches. He ain't rude. He's just honest-- very honest. How else would you want your teacher to be?

So I realized why kids weren't piling into the room to jam with Scott. The same reason I had never done it. FEAR!!! One day recently I had an hour to kill, and Scott's room was empty, save for one young student to whom Scott was giving some encouragement. I took a deep breath, grabbed my new Knaggs Kenai guitar and sat down on one of the many amps in the room. Nervous! I told myself I'd never forgive myself for never sitting in with the great Scott Henderson when I had the opportunity. He asked what I wanted to do, and I said right away, " I'm a rock guitar player and I'm really weak on Jazz." He said "Great, let's play some Blues!" He punched up a 12 bar Blues loop on his laptop- in G - and off we went. He took his solos to places I never could have imagined, while still sounding bluesy, nasty and rockin'! I'm not a big fan of Jazz, but when its done in a Rock and Blues context I can more easily get into it. And Scott is the master. It's in a language I understand. When I played, I just did... well, my thing. I'll admit, just to show I could jazz it up a little, I threw a few altered scale runs here and there, including one I learned from an old Scott Henderson video. He totally caught it and nodded to me like "... Yeah, thats right!" Cool! We played for about an hour.

When we finished jamming, he started unplugging his stuff and he complimented my tone. He really liked the way my Knaggs sounded, and was quick to say he knows it's all in the hands, but that he could tell it was a great guitar. He stood up and shook my hand, and was very kind with a couple more compliments, and said I was welcome anytime I wanted...

To my surprise, I felt quite at ease and unintimidated while we played. In the end, it didn't matter how knowledgeable I was or wasn't about music, which college I went to, how many standards I could play, etc., etc. It wasn't a highly trained, mega genius- Jazz Fusion icon and some slush Rock guitar player (me). It was just two guitar players; two musicians playing the Blues... doing what we love to do, each bringing our own voice and expression.
What a cool experience! What a cool and generous musician Scott is. The great ones usually are.

*ref: Tribal Tech (Fusion band co-founded by Scott Henderson)
www.scotthenderson.net

# Rod DeGeorge

## Play What You Mean, Mean What You Play

. . .

*Tools for Creating Authentic Music - Volume IIII*

Welcome to Volume four of,Play What You mean, Mean What You Play. In this issue we are going discuss one of the more effective ways, at least in my opinion, to help you get familiar withthe specific feels or colors of different chord and scale tones.

By fully understandingand internalizing how a certain chord or scale tone feels, you can express yourself in a more authentic way. For example, if you are trying to create tension or release to accentuate a lyric, a developedunderstandingof how to convey that emotion through music, will be more effective than trial and error. You won't have to settle for something close to what you intendedif you understandhow each chord or scale tone feels.

*Rod DeGeorge, session guitarist and solo artist*

Try singing or humming a certain chord or scale tone as you play the chord on your guitar. For example, play a C chord and sing the root (C). Try to feel the vibration of the guitar against your body, and feel how that C vibrates in your head and/or chest. Now feel the relationship between the vibrations of the note that you are singing and the chord that you are playing. Do the same with the 3rd (E), in this case it is a major third, and then the 5th (G).

They each have a distinct feel or color to them. Also try this with a C minor chord (C, Eb, G) and you should be able to experience the difference of the minor 3rd as opposed to the major 3rd, as it will convey a much different feel.

When doing this, I don't suggest trying to memorize the pitch as much as trying to experience the relationship of the note with the chord. This is not as much of an intellectual attribute as it is an emotional one, if that makes sense.

To take this exercise even further, try strumming the C major chord and sing the 4th (F) then resolve to the 3rd (E). Do this again but now resolve up to the 5th (G).Now try singing the major 6th (A) over the C chord and resolve down to the 5th. Then the major 7th (B) and resolve up to the root (C). Feel the tension and release. The 4th has a different feel or pull than the 6th or the 7th. They all create unique feels. Finally, turn this C chord into a Dominant chord by singing the b7th (Bb) and resolving up to the root (C). Now the 9th (D) and resolve to the root. As you can see, you can do this with any chord and scale to help internalize the feel or color.

I have always felt that it is better to learn by experiencing first hand, than to try to memorize someone else's description of their experience. This is why I try not to apply too many adjectives when talking about the feel of a certain chord, scale, interval etc. What I consider suspensefulordramatic, may be different than what you consider suspenseful or dramatic. You Dig?

This application can be very useful when someone, who may have a lot of technical ability,can rip up and down the fretboard, but still struggles to improvise a slow melodic line. On a number of occasions, various students of mine haveshown rapid improvement in their improvisational and compositional skills, as well as their confidence, after doing similar exercises as the ones mentioned here. Hearing where you are, and knowing where you want to go (and how to get there), is when you can create authentic music. Just knowing what scales work over what chords, and having the ability to rip through them, doesn't always mean you are creating music that will touch someone.

I hope this was helpful in some way, or at least interesting. Until next time...
Peace,
Rod

www.degeorgemusic.com

# Guitar Connoisseur

## Back Issues

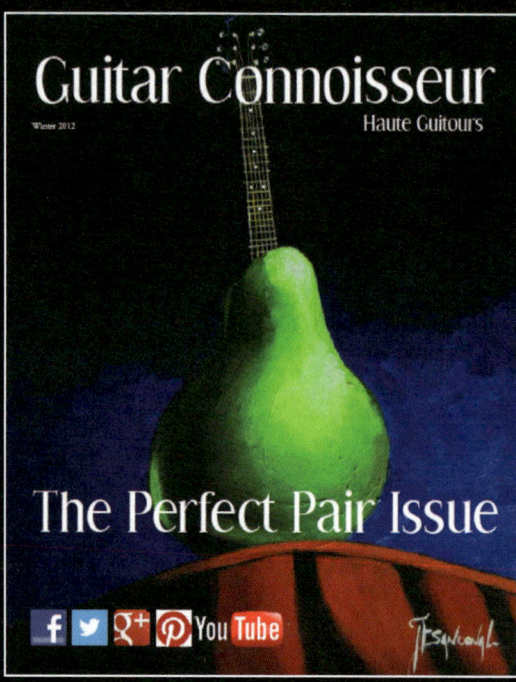

CPSIA information can be obtained
at www.ICGtesting.com
Printed in the USA
LVIW02n1422160913
352673LV00047B